The Power of Unreasonable People

LEADERSHIP <small>FOR THE</small>
COMMON GOOD

HARVARD BUSINESS PRESS

CENTER FOR PUBLIC LEADERSHIP
JOHN F. KENNEDY SCHOOL OF GOVERNMENT
HARVARD UNIVERSITY

The Leadership for the Common Good series represents a
partnership between Harvard Business Press and the
Center for Public Leadership at Harvard University's
John F. Kennedy School of Government. Books in the series
aim to provoke conversations about the role of leaders in
business, government, and society, to enrich leadership theory
and enhance leadership practice, and to set the agenda for
defining effective leadership in the future.

OTHER BOOKS IN THE SERIES

Changing Minds
by Howard Gardner

Predictable Surprises
by Max H. Bazerman and
Michael D. Watkins

Bad Leadership
by Barbara Kellerman

Many Unhappy Returns
by Charles O. Rossotti

Leading Through Conflict
by Mark Gerzon

Five Minds for the Future
by Howard Gardner

The Leaders We Need
by Michael Maccoby

Through the Labyrinth
by Alice H. Eagly and
Linda L. Carli

Followership
by Barbara Kellerman

The Power of Unreasonable People

How Social Entrepreneurs Create Markets

That Change the World

John Elkington • Pamela Hartigan

HARVARD BUSINESS PRESS

Boston, Massachusetts

Library of Congress Cataloging-in-Publication Data
    Elkington, John.
    The power of unreasonable people : how social entrepreneurs create
markets that change the world / John Elkington and Pamela Hartigan.
        p.   cm.
    Includes bibliographical references and index.
    ISBN-13: 978-1-4221-0406-4
    1. Social entrepreneurship. 2. Social change. I. Hartigan, Pamela.
    HD60.E45 2008
    361.7068'8—dc22
                                                    2007030382

CONTENTS

Part III: Leading Sustainable and Scalable Change

Thanks to this book and its catchy title, I imagine that we will soon see a host of people claiming to be "unreasonable." If so, the world may end up better off. The characteristics of the "unreasonable" men and women whom John Elkington and Pamela Hartigan describe are exactly the characteristics that our world needs during times of profound transformation.

It is extraordinary how much this agenda has evolved. When my wife Hilde and I created the Schwab Foundation for Social Entrepreneurship in 1998, the notion of "social entrepreneurship" was almost unheard of in Europe and little known in the rest of the world, despite Ashoka's pioneering efforts. Indeed, when we registered the Schwab Foundation in Switzerland, we faced the challenge of translating the term social entrepreneurship, not then in the French and German lexicons.

No one did more to open our eyes to the potential than Muhammad Yunus. In the early 1970s, he began his tireless work to prove that poor women are creditworthy. Yet, the world took more than thirty years to fully recognize the value of micro-credit. How many more "unreasonable" people like Yunus are out there?, we wondered. Hundreds, perhaps thousands. We began to convene some of the world's most influential social entrepreneurs, who pointed us to three critical needs:

- Legitimacy for their "unreasonable" models
- Access to networks of political, business, and media leaders
- Capital

But we did not have enough capital to meet the needs of the social entrepreneurs whom we were convening. We quickly concluded, however, that we could offer something as important—access to the World Economic Forum. So, the foundation worked to identify the most innovative social entrepreneurs and, in collaboration with the forum, to showcase their proved, practical solutions to economic, social, and environmental challenges. Our annual summits, where the Schwab Foundation's growing community of 115 entrepreneurs gathers, are a hotbed of such exchanges. Today, well over half are working together to "import" or "export" their methods and technologies among their organizations across geographical and political boundaries.

Meanwhile, a multitude of related institutions and activities has mushroomed around the globe, and a number of well-endowed foundations have sprung up to support entrepreneurship in the public interest. International gatherings such as the Skoll World Forum draw thousands, and benefactors have created multiple prizes, including national awards spearheaded by the Schwab Foundation in some thirty countries.

We are immensely proud that Pamela Hartigan has led the foundation during this historic shift and that John Elkington has been closely involved with us since the organization's inception. When we first introduced social entrepreneurs at the World Economic Forum's Annual Meeting in 2002 at a session entitled "Come Meet the Social Entrepreneurs," scarcely anyone turned up—and those who did mainly wanted to meet our board members, including composer Quincy Jones, storyteller Paulo Coelho, and film producer David Puttnam. Today, we have fully integrated social entrepreneurs into the forum program; corporate leaders court them for their ideas, insights, and innovations, and the international media eagerly follow their stories. You will meet many of them here. Clearly, the power exists; the challenge now is to harness it to drive the necessary scale of change.

—Professor Klaus Schwab
Founder and Executive Chairman, World Economic Forum

First, a word or two about our title. "The reasonable man adapts himself to the world," playwright George Bernard Shaw once said, whereas "the unreasonable one persists in trying to adapt the world to himself. Therefore all progress depends on the unreasonable man."[1] By this definition, not only are most of the entrepreneurs described in the following pages unreasonable—many have actually been dubbed "crazy," even by family and friends—but a large slice of the future may hinge on their success in spreading their apparently unhinged ideas and business models.

It is clear that the world faces epochal challenges—from outright conflict, terrorism, and weapons of mass destruction; to poverty and hunger; to the threat of global pandemics and, perhaps the biggest issue of all, climate change. But, tackled in the right way, today's crises will lead to tomorrow's solutions, and the size of the potential market opportunities is staggering.

There are an estimated 4 billion low-income consumers, constituting a majority of the world's population, and they make up what is called the "base of the (economic) pyramid," or BOP. An ever-expanding body of research is exploring how to use market-based approaches to "better meet their needs, increase their productivity and incomes, and empower their entry into the formal economy."[2] BOP markets are far from small: it is estimated, for example, that the BOP market in Asia (and the Mid-East regions) is made up of 2.86 billion people with a total income of $3.47 trillion. In Eastern Europe it is estimated at $458 billion; in Latin

America, $509 billion; and in Africa, $429 billion.[3] In total, these markets are thought to be worth some $5 trillion.

But how can mainstream business, financial, and political leaders best come to grips with these emerging trends in value creation? Three answers immediately spring to mind. First, they can experiment with new business models, as much of the BOP literature suggests. Second, as leading business thinkers have long argued, a can-do attitude is much more likely to succeed than don't-do, won't-do, or can't-do mind-sets. And, third, it makes sense to track down, study, and work alongside can-do and we-can-work-out-how-to-do-it innovators and entrepreneurs who are already hard at work on developing real-world solutions. That is what the two of us have been doing since the turn of the millennium—identifying, studying, networking, and supporting some of the world's most successful social and environmental entrepreneurs.

Although there is new momentum, this is not a new field of inquiry. Among the books already published are excellent works with titles like *How to Change the World*, *Profits with Principles*, and *Untapped*—the last of which is subtitled "Creating Value in Underserved Markets."[4] But we hope to bring new perspectives and insights to bear. As noted in our acknowledgments, *The Power of Unreasonable People* results from a close working relationship between SustainAbility (founded in 1987 and now based in London; Washington, D.C.; and Zurich) and the Schwab Foundation for Social Entrepreneurship (founded in 1998 and based in Geneva).

SustainAbility's work in this area has also been helped by the award in 2006 of a three-year $1 million grant from the Skoll Foundation, established by eBay cofounder Jeff Skoll. That said, anything like global sustainability will be impossible without the engagement—and radical restructuring—of business and markets. As Jeff Skoll's ex-colleague Pierre Omidyar put it, "I have learnt that if you want to have a global impact you can't ignore business. I don't mean corporate responsibility programs, but business models that provoke social change."[5]

So where can such changes and change agents be found? Time and again during periods of extraordinary volatility, disruption, and change, the best place to look for clues to tomorrow's revolutionary business models is at the fringes of the current dysfunctional system, so that's where we headed. The journey has taken us from the mainstream to the margins—from the Alpine meetings of the global elite in Davos and gatherings of social entrepreneurs in places like São Paulo to the festering waste dumps of Bangladesh; from top business schools to violence-torn countries in the Middle East and HIV-plagued communities across Africa. In the process, we believe that we have found clues to the ways in which all businesses—large or small, corporate or entrepreneurial—will operate in tomorrow's markets.

   —John Elkington and Pamela Hartigan
      London and Geneva
      October 1, 2007

ACKNOWLEDGMENTS

The Power of Unreasonable People has involved a much longer journey than either of us originally imagined. Our families, friends, and colleagues could be forgiven for considering the project an unreasonable incursion. But the upside has been that our thinking—and, with it, this book—has had to evolve.

In retrospect, *The Power of Unreasonable People* forms part of a trilogy, beginning in 1997 with the first publication of *Cannibals with Forks*.[1] This book brought the notion of multidimensional value creation—and the term *triple bottom line*—to a wider audience, mainly businesspeople but also some of the entrepreneurs profiled here.[2] The book focused on some of the processes by which economic, social, and environmental value can be created—or destroyed. *The Chrysalis Economy*, the second book in the trilogy, explored some of the ways in which—to use a term coined by our friend and colleague Jed Emerson—new forms of "blended value" can be created.[3] Published in 2001, *The Chrysalis Economy* predicted a period of profound creative destruction in the global economy, most intensively through 2000–2030.

That same year that the second book was published, we first met at a summit on social entrepreneurship held at the World Economic Forum and hosted by the Schwab Foundation. We began formal work on what would become *The Power of Unreasonable People* a couple of years later. The book introduces and evaluates some of the most interesting entrepreneurs we have had the pleasure to meet and, in a number of instances, work with. A key part of our purpose is to better connect these people with mainstream markets, businesses, and financial institutions.

Recalling and thanking everyone who contributed directly or indirectly to *The Power of Unreasonable People* would be a Herculean task. Having visited hundreds of entrepreneurs and companies around the world, and talked to literally thousands of people, it is impossible to rewind and acknowledge all the conversations and events that have shaped our thinking.

Take, as an example, the breakfast one of us had with Hervé Houdré, general manager of one of Washington, D.C.'s, best-known institutions, the Willard Hotel. When he heard what we were doing, he steered us across the street to a nearby Borders bookshop and ensured that we tracked down a copy of Walter Isaacson's stunning biography of one of the most extraordinary social entrepreneurs of all time: Benjamin Franklin.[4] Houdré—who has led the charge in greening the Willard and the wider InterContinental Hotels Group—also underscores a central theme of the book: entrepreneurial solutions to the world's greatest challenges are being developed in major global businesses, not just in small-scale social enterprises. And both sides, we argue, have a huge amount to learn from the other.

The Power of Unreasonable People has been an open source project.[5] That said, many of those whose wisdom, expertise, and experience we have drawn on are mentioned in the text and in the references section at the end of the book. To further signal and acknowledge those wider debts, we would like to thank four groups of people without whose support the book would not have been possible—at least, not in anything like its current form.

First of all, our sincere thanks go to Professor Klaus and Hilde Schwab for creating the Schwab Foundation—and for opening up the workings of the World Economic Forum, which they also founded, to social entrepreneurs. We also acknowledge the debt we owe to the foundation's other board members: Stephen Brenninkmeijer, business entrepreneur and head of the United Kingdom's Andromeda Fund; best-selling author Paulo Coelho; David Gergen, director of the Center for Public Leadership at Harvard

University; composer Quincy Jones; Zanele Mbeki, South Africa's first lady; Lord David Puttnam, former chairman of the United Kingdom's National Endowment for Science, Technology and the Arts; and Muhammad Yunus, founder and managing director of the Grameen Bank in Bangladesh. We also thank the Schwab Foundation's Mirjam Schöning, Parag Gupta, Kevin Teo, and Sandor Nagy, a great team of colleagues whose constant work makes a difference to social and environmental entrepreneurship globally.

Second, our thanks go to five other groups that played key roles in supporting *The Power of Unreasonable People*: Sustain-Ability (particularly Seb Beloe, Maggie Brenneke, Ritu Khanna, Sam Lakha, Mark Lee, Geoff Lye, Kavita Prakash-Mani, Sophia Tickell, and Peter Zollinger—plus SustainAbility faculty members Jed Emerson of Generation Investment Management, Peter Kinder of KLD, Jane Nelson of Harvard's Kennedy School of Government, and Jan-Olaf Willums of InSpire Invest); the World Economic Forum, especially André Schneider and Ged Davis (who has since retired from the forum but is actively involved in the renewable energy industry); the DSM Agency (especially Doris Michaels and Delia Fakis), which has enthusiastically and professionally represented the book and helped us improve the manuscript in a number of ways; and Harvard Business Press, our publishers (particularly Astrid Sandoval, to whom—alongside George Bernard Shaw—we owe our title, and Kirsten Sandberg, Jennifer Waring, Ania Wieckowski, Carolyn Monaco, Michelle Morgan, Daisy Hutton, Zeenat Potia, and Sarah Mann); and Colleen Kaftan and Lorry Maggio, who helped us run the last quarter mile. SustainAbility also gratefully acknowledges the generous three-year funding it received in 2006 from the Skoll Foundation, with particular thanks to Jeff Skoll and Sally Osberg. Thanks, too, to Sandy Herz, Rowena Young, and Andrea Westall for their help in building our involvement in the Skoll World Forums.

Third, we want to express our huge admiration of—and appreciation for—the social entrepreneurs and their many investors and supporters, without whom this book would have been impossible. Many are referenced in the following pages, but for a fuller sense of who is now involved, we recommend visiting www.ashoka.org, www.schwabfound.org, and www.skollfoundation.org. For further background, we recommend the work of David Bornstein, especially *How to Change the World*.

Fourth and finally, honoring our most heartfelt debts, we dedicate the book to our families: Elaine, Gaia, and Hania Elkington; and Martin, Emilie, and Jesse Hartigan. They have made contributions too numerous and too diverse to mention. This book has benefited from an array of conversations over several years, many of them with those dearest to us. We hope they will think that the journey has been worth the adventures to date—and that they will be happy to embark with us on the next leg.

Roots of Unreason, Sources of Power

B EING UNREASONABLE is not just a state of mind. It is also a process by which older, outdated forms of reasoning are jettisoned and new ones conceived and evolved. As the process unfolds, those mired in the older, obsolete paradigms can become threatened by—and aggressive toward—the innovators, particularly if those innovators move into the mainstream worlds of business, finance, and politics. But like it or not, the world is in the early stages of powerful, deep-running, and pervasive changes that, for better or worse, will transform its economies, its cultures, and people's understanding of who they are and what they stand for.

Our intention in what follows is simple: to introduce a new generation of social and environmental entrepreneurs and to investigate the relevance of their thinking about value creation, their business models, and their leadership styles for mainstream decision makers. We include many predictions and observations from the entrepreneurs themselves, culled from hundreds of hours of interviews, personal conversations, and direct collaboration over decades of intensive work in related areas.

These social and environmental entrepreneurs lead by example. They attack intractable problems, take huge risks, and force the rest of us to look beyond the edge of what seems possible. They seek outlandish goals, such as economic and environmental sustainability and social equity, often aiming to transform the systems whose dysfunctions help create or aggravate major socioeconomic, environmental, or political problems. In so doing, they uncover new ways to disrupt established industries while creating new paths for the future.

Global corporations are now scouting for high-impact social and environmental entrepreneurs. Why? They give three main reasons. First, market intelligence (these entrepreneurs are seen as highly sensitive barometers for detecting market risks and opportunities). Second, retention and development of talent (a growing number of companies, like Accenture, say that offering the opportunity to work alongside accomplished entrepreneurs factors into staff retention, as well as professional development). And, third, as one CEO at a recent Davos summit candidly put it, "It is nice to be seen with people who are loved."

All this should come with a clear caveat, however: as in any field of entrepreneurship, many of these people will fail, and some will fail repeatedly as they tackle tough challenges. But periods of great change are built on intense experimentation and, often, high failure rates. Our reading of the evidence suggests that the work of these innovators and entrepreneurs heralds a new phase in the evolution of business, markets, and capitalism itself. The mainstream players who heed the lessons from these innovators' experience will find new opportunities to fulfill unmet needs in the vast underserved markets of the twenty-first century.

Think of it this way: whatever they may intend, these entrepreneurs are doing early market research on some of the biggest opportunities of the coming decades. In attempting to bridge the great divides between privileged populations and the poor, they address the critical challenges where traditional markets fail. But, as we shall see, they cannot tackle market failures on their own. Instead, their efforts need to be supported by all levels of government, by business, by the financial markets, and by civil society's organizations and ordinary citizens—that is, by each and every one of us. We outline some necessary actions for key sectors in the conclusion.

Who Are These Social and Environmental Entrepreneurs?

There is no standard-issue entrepreneur, but there is a consensus on what entrepreneurs do. Through the practical exploitation of new ideas, they establish new ventures to deliver goods and services not currently supplied by existing markets. Social and environmental entrepreneurs share the same characteristics as all entrepreneurs—namely, they are innovative, resourceful, practical, and opportunistic. They delight in coming up with new products or services, or new approaches to delivering products or services to existing or previously undiscovered markets. What motivates many of these people is not doing the "deal" but achieving the "ideal." And because the ideal takes a lot longer to realize, these entrepreneurs tend to be in the game for the long haul, not just until they can sell their venture to the highest bidder.

Social and environmental entrepreneurs operate across a spectrum of enterprises, from the purely charitable to the purely commercial.[1] But because many of the markets they address are immature, they tend to skew toward the nonprofit end.

On the purely charitable side, "customers" pay little or nothing, capital comes in the form of donations and grants, the workforce is largely made up of volunteers, and suppliers make in-kind donations. At the purely commercial end of the spectrum, by contrast, most transactions are at market rates. Many of the most interesting experiments take place in the middle ground, however, where hybrid organizations pursue new forms of *blended value* and where better-off customers sometimes subsidize less well-off customers. Blended value is what results when businesses—whether for-profit or nonprofit—create value in multiple dimensions—economic, social and environmental. So a key challenge for twenty-first-century investors and managers will be to boost the attractiveness to all key stakeholders of the value blends they create.[2]

One burning question that invariably comes up, particularly when successful business entrepreneurs meet successful social entrepreneurs, is "What motivates you?" The implication behind the question is "If you have been so clever in achieving what you have accomplished, why haven't you applied your talents to making money?" In response to that question, David Green, one of the world's outstanding examples of entrepreneurial brilliance applied to creating financial models that deliver quality health technologies to the world's poorest, quipped: "My reasons are purely selfish. I figure I have been put on this earth for a very short period of time. I could apply my talents to making lots of money, but where would I be at the end of my lifetime? I would much rather be remembered for having made a significant contribution to improving the world into which I came than for having made millions."[3]

Against this motivational backdrop, social entrepreneurs develop and operate new ventures that prioritize social returns on investment. For example, they aim to improve the quality of life for marginalized populations in terms of poverty, health, or education and attempt to achieve higher leverage than conventional philanthropy and nongovernmental organizations. "Ten Characteristics of Social Entrepreneurs" lists other characteristics they tend to have in common.

Many consider environmental entrepreneurship to be a subset of social entrepreneurship, but the environmental entrepreneurs generally see themselves as a distinct group. For one thing, they tend to operate on the for-profit end of the enterprise spectrum. Beginning in 2002, the sector has gravitated toward a major rebranding as the clean technology, or "cleantech," industry, driven by the eponymous Cleantech Group.[4]

Ten Characteristics of Successful Social Entrepreneurs

WHAT CHARACTERISTICS do these social and environmental entrepreneurs share?

Capturing the common characteristics of such extraordinary, diverse people is tough, but here are some especially noteworthy qualities. Among other things, these entrepreneurs:

- Try to shrug off the constraints of ideology or discipline

- Identify and apply practical solutions to social problems, combining innovation, resourcefulness, and opportunity

- Innovate by finding a new product, a new service, or a new approach to a social problem

- Focus—first and foremost—on social value creation and, in that spirit, are willing to share their innovations and insights for others to replicate

- Jump in before ensuring they are fully resourced

- Have an unwavering belief in everyone's innate capacity, often regardless of education, to contribute meaningfully to economic and social development

- Show a dogged determination that pushes them to take risks that others wouldn't dare

- Balance their passion for change with a zeal to measure and monitor their impact

- Have a great deal to teach change makers in other sectors

- Display a healthy impatience (e.g., they don't do well in bureaucracies, which can raise succession issues as their organizations grow—and almost inevitably become more bureaucratic)

But as interest grows in trying to solve the world's great social, environmental, and governance challenges, the definitions—and the boundaries between fields—blur. In the process, the field of social entrepreneurship has become "a truly immense tent into which all manner of socially beneficial activities may fit," as two board members of the Skoll Foundation—Roger Martin, dean of the Rotman School of Management, and Sally Osberg, the foundation's president and CEO—put it.[5] One result, inevitably, is confusion. So, they argue, the real measure of social entrepreneurship should be "direct action that generates a paradigm shift in the way a societal need is met." What such people do, in effect, is to identify and attack an "unsatisfactory equilibrium." Their endeavors are transformative, not palliative, with the power to catalyze and shape the future. And, once you know where to look, you find them at work almost everywhere, as described in the appendix.

What Makes Them Unreasonable?

A few years ago, Muhammad Yunus—the world's leading social entrepreneur, founder of the revolutionary Grameen Bank, pioneer of microfinance, and winner of the 2006 Nobel Peace Prize—described his breed to us as "70 percent crazy." It's extraordinary how often his fellow entrepreneurs have told us that they have been called crazy by the media, by colleagues, by friends, and even by family members. But they are crazy like the proverbial fox. They look for—and often find—solutions to insoluble problems in the unlikeliest places. They are driven by a passion to expand business thinking to reach people in need. Thus, many are pioneering and helping map out future markets where most of us would only see nightmarish problems and risk.

From Social Activist to Disruptive Innovator:
Orlando Rincón Bonilla

Consider Orlando Rincón Bonilla and his nonprofit model designed to bootstrap poor communities into the twenty-first century. Mention his native Colombia, and the drug cartels, guerillas, and paramilitary are among the first things that come to mind. A youngster growing up poor in this beautiful Andean country might seem to have only those three options before him. But Colombia is nothing if not a country of contrasts, and it was in the very barrios that feed criminal activity that Rincón was born.

One of ten siblings from a poor family in Cali, he grew up feeling the sting of both poverty and exclusion.[6] As a teenager, he became a leftist activist and joined a youth organization run through his neighborhood church. The priest named him president of the association, but Rincón refused to even set foot in the building. He didn't want to be constrained by organizational expectations, including those of the Catholic Church. Instead, the group met in the park— the center of community life. His political activism soon earned him a reputation. It also cost him a place at the public university but, in the process, opened up other opportunities. He won a scholarship and attended the University of Medellín, which was particularly surprising given that, as a private university, it was geared to educate the sons of the elite, most of them businessmen.

Rincón's studies in systems engineering marked a turning point. The exposure to other ways of thinking influenced his own, convincing him that ideology alone was not the answer. With a double specialization in engineering and anthropology and a passion for mathematics, he gravitated to computer science and software. So did one of his university classmates, William Corredor. In 1984, the two decided to go into the software business. They created Open Systems, a private company that makes software products and services for fixed and mobile telephone networks as well as for the cable television, Internet, domestic gas, electricity, and drinking water sectors.

Fifteen years later, Rincón had become wealthier than he could ever have imagined, but he was not happy. He was uneasy with what seemed to be the inescapable tension between maximizing profits and prioritizing his country's social development needs. He believed deeply in the innovative capacity of his fellow Colombians. One question in particular troubled him: what model would allow

Colombia to grow economically without compromising the values of justice and equity to which Rincón was firmly committed?

He went in search of the answers. First, he visited India to see how this country had managed to transform itself into a global leader in information technology services, but he did not find entrepreneurs. Rather, he found managers and millions of workers, all contracted by large national and international companies whose executives lived in comfortable neighborhoods in Delhi, Bangalore, Los Angeles, New York, and London. Rincón interpreted what he saw as a new form of slavery justified by the rationale that these workers were earning somewhat better salaries than they would have received in the local market. Moreover, he was troubled by what he saw as the forced Americanization of the workers, who were able to advance their careers to the degree that they spoke English "like a Yank" and had adopted American-sounding names.

From India he went to Ireland. Perhaps the secret to Colombia's economic and social development lay there? After all, Ireland had been touted as one of the hot spots for competitive industries, including IT. Despite the tremendous affinity Rincón developed for the people there, the Irish miracle he discovered was akin to a large *maquiladora* for multinational corporations such as IBM and Microsoft. It seemed that there was little or no indigenous IT entrepreneurial activity—it had all been imported from abroad. For Rincón, whatever model Colombia followed would have to recognize the ingenuity and capacity of Colombians and to stimulate, wherever possible, their ability to be entrepreneurial, self-employed, and independent. Upon his return, he decided to invest his fortune in boosting entrepreneurialism and, in the process, changing Colombian society.

His stake in Open Systems, a leading technology solutions provider based in Colombia with 10 million customers across six Latin American countries and 2004 revenues of $14 million, had made him independently wealthy. In 1999, he left Open Systems—although he still owns a stake in the company—and started Parque-Soft. "Once I found my way, I wanted to generate a shortcut for many intelligent, educated, poor young people so that they could generate companies of their own and create new leadership for our society," he explains.[7] "So instead of spending my money on luxuries or vices, I began to invest in people in the belief that my money could be useful to others like me."

ParqueSoft is a nonprofit innovation park that draws budding software enthusiasts from poor communities. Within five years, it grew into a network of twelve technology centers in as many major Colombian cities in the Valle del Cauca, the southwest corridor of the country. The network houses two hundred software companies, comprising some twelve hundred workers, about 75 percent of whom are young entrepreneurs.

ParqueSoft is not a traditional incubator, however. Once an enterprise has reached a determined size and turnover, it does not leave ParqueSoft; the young people who create and develop their companies at ParqueSoft want to stay and keep growing. They also welcome new entrepreneurs who join the fold and benefit from the extraordinary leverage that comes from belonging to a dynamic, creative community where talent and know-how can solve the most complicated problems that are brought to bear from clients all over the world.

Each of ParqueSoft's offices is a beehive of activity. Within a large open space, enterprises are organized into blocks, depending on the size of the team. Each team is a software company that designs, develops, and sells many different types of software, including optics, artificial intelligence, edutainment, bioinformatics, and nanotechnology tools. These companies currently sell their software in over forty countries. The open-space system allows for continuous informal exchanges within and between companies. ParqueSoft has created an ecosystem that stimulates innovation, inquiry, and the improvement of software products for sale to national and international clients.

Yet anyone who thinks that ParqueSoft is mainly about information technology businesses is mistaken. "ParqueSoft is a social initiative that happens to use science and technology as a vehicle," Rincón explains. "Its objective is to stimulate democracy and social justice through the inclusion of previously marginalized young people living in low-income communities, transforming them into protagonists of their own enterprises, not employees."

With a head of wild curly hair and a uniform of open shirts and jeans, Orlando Rincón Bonilla could easily be mistaken for one of the entrepreneurs at ParqueSoft. He is brilliant without being arrogant, frequently irreverent, and very funny. Most of all, he loves the young people with whom he works. On the day we spent at one of the ParqueSoft sites, we had many questions: "How can you be sure that the entrepreneurs that grow their ventures at ParqueSoft will also be committed to their communities' development? What if all they want is to become as wealthy as possible and forget about being good corporate citizens?"

Within minutes, Rincón assembles a group of about twenty young men and women working in various ventures housed on the third floor of the building. He asks them the same questions. All of them start speaking animatedly and at once. An hour into the conversation, it is clear that these young people are not waiting to become successful before becoming involved in their communities. They are already involved almost as fully as they are in growing their own ventures.

Rincón is a tough act to follow, so any question of succession seems irrelevant. Nonetheless, he has set up ParqueSoft to function well without him, fully run by a council of entrepreneurs elected by the collectivity. His succession plan has been delineated from the outset, in part by how he chose the entrepreneurs who came to ParqueSoft initially and now form part of its council. Rincón is a firm believer that entrepreneurs are born, not made. "It's genetic," he frequently says. "You can walk into a room full of people and pick the entrepreneurs out in seconds. It's something about the look in their eyes." What, then, is it that makes these people seem so unreasonable?

They're Unreasonable Because They Want to Change the System

Look around, and the world is full of unsatisfactory equilibriums that entrepreneurs like Rincón love to disrupt. We are very likely in the early stages of the greatest periods of creative destruction in our global economy. Social and environmental entrepreneurs are not the answer to all our prayers, but they signal some of the ways in which we can steer the processes of change.

Their power derives from the fact that they spot dysfunction in the current system, and, unlike reasonable people who accommodate themselves to the status quo, they try to work out how to transition the system equilibrium to a different—and more functional—state.

Coming decades will require unprecedented levels of system change, so we had better listen to the unreasonable entrepreneurs who are exploring when, where, and how to effect change. In this spirit, some leading funders are already trying to identify and support social and environmental entrepreneurs. For example, the Schwab Foundation for Social Entrepreneurship has joined forces with the Lemelson Foundation to establish the Leapfrog Fund, designed to spur the transfer of successful innovations between entrepreneurs in different parts of the world. Such replication is one key part of system change, but another is altering the system conditions, the strategy adopted by would-be game changers like those behind the transparency, accountability, and emission-trading movements we will discuss in later chapters. The risks of relative failure with such wildly ambitious goals are much greater, but the payoffs are also likely to be proportionately greater.

They're Unreasonable Because They Are Insanely Ambitious

It's true, many of them are insanely ambitious. That is what makes them so interesting—and potentially transformative. They are can-do thinkers, frustrated by the don't-do, can't-do, and won't-do people they often find themselves confronting. But ambition often gets a bad rap. The difference is that these entrepreneurs' ambition is not about them; it is about achieving for the benefit of a far greater goal. Think of 2004 Nobel Peace Laureate Wangari Maathai of East Africa's Green Belt Movement and her insanely ambitious plan to plant 15 million trees. Her supplier never believed that she was serious; he wasn't even close to being able to deliver the number of trees he had promised as she got started. Now, with 30 million trees planted, Maathai and her colleagues talk about ultimately planting 1 billion trees, moving far beyond their initial efforts in Kenya. As the then president (and despot) Daniel Arap Moi must have sometimes wondered, is there no stopping the woman?

They're Unreasonable Because They Are Propelled by Emotion

Whether or not we admit it, we are all fueled by emotion to some degree. That said, you find, time and again, that these entrepreneurs have had a life-transforming experience, some sort of an epiphany, that launched them on their current mission. They may be deeply concerned—even angry—about the loss of biodiversity, about the treatment of ethnic minorities, or about the fact that 750 million people worldwide are illiterate and that 100 million children have no chance of going to school. But their passion and the experiences that originally turned them on to the cause do not make them crazy—at least, not in the clinical sense. Among those who have reported some form of conversion experience are people as diverse as Bob Geldof, Bono, Fazle Abed of BRAC, Bunker Roy of Barefoot College, Roy Prosterman of the Rural Development Institute, and, in the corporate mainstream, Wal-Mart CEO Lee Scott (whose transformative experience came in the wake of Hurricane Katrina).

Yes, some of these people get angry—as we all should when faced with the challenges they are trying to spotlight and get decision makers to tackle. What is different is that their anger, their passion, isn't simply blown away as steam. Instead, they work out how to turn it into useful locomotion. In the process, they have to strike a balance between passion and effective change. People Tree, for example, is a social enterprise that directs 10 percent of the profits from its ethical fashion collection to promoting awareness of the fair trade agenda. Founder Safia Minney notes that sophisticated consumers may recoil from in-your-face campaigns, so most of People Tree's designs do not include messaging or slogans; they instead provide information with the use instructions and packaging, what Minney dubs "subtle education." As such pioneers evolve effective new marketing and communication strategies, the potential for others to move into the resulting opportunity spaces could grow exponentially.

They're Unreasonable Because They Think They Know the Future

At a time when most of us are confused and uncertain about what the future might hold, leading social entrepreneurs brim over with confidence. They know that the best way to predict the future is to create it and the best way to build momentum—and attract funding and other resources—is to develop and communicate a clear vision of how things might be different. These entrepreneurs see a bigger picture, sometimes mulling it over for decades. For them, Winston Churchill's adage that the further you can see back, the further you can see forward holds true.

Anyone looking for clues on how to spur innovation and creativity in the real world should listen to David Galenson, the economist whose work in this area started pretty much by accident. He was spurred to wonder—while bidding for a painting at auction—about links between the age of artists at the time they create a piece of artwork and its subsequent fame and price at auction.[8] This led him to what some have described as the "unified field theory of creativity," distinguishing between two broad types of innovators.

Conceptual innovators are revolutionaries, break with the past, are blessed with certainty, know what they want, and tend to bloom early, like Picasso in painting, Mozart in music, and Orson Welles in film. *Experimental innovators*, by contrast, include people like Cézanne in art, Beethoven in music, and Alfred Hitchcock in film. They tend to proceed in fits and starts, work endlessly to perfect their technique, move slowly toward goals they don't totally understand, and as a result, never know when a work is finished. Interestingly, many experimental innovators—including great entrepreneurs like

Edison and Ford—didn't die early.[9] Instead, they tinkered on into ripe old age.

As Galenson explored the patterns of creativity in others areas, such as architecture and economics, he began to realize that these two fundamental types of genius could be found across all forms of human creativity and endeavor. Over time, too, he came to understand that innovators aren't either conceptual or experimental, but that they can be located along a continuum, with conceptual innovators at one end and experimental innovators at the other. As he dug deeper, he concluded that since economic activity is all about value creation, then investors, companies, governments, and business schools need to wake up to these differences and support both types of innovators.

The entrepreneurs we profile are all very much experimental in how they operate, but most are also conceptual thinkers. They are also optimists, confident that it is possible to change the world for the better. And, again, they are ambitious. "I think the ultimate challenge of sustainable business," HydroGen president Joshua Tosteson explained during an Investors' Circle survey, "is how to undercut the compelling advantages of economies of scale with quality-focused business models. In 10 years' time, there will be no distinction between a 'social venture' and most major businesses— it will be a *sine qua non* of business going forward."[10]

At their best, such people see things others do not. They draw conclusions that others cannot. They instinctively reframe challenges as opportunities, looking well beyond today's horizons. In the process, they offer those in the mainstream a way of getting a glimpse of the social and environmental drivers that will shape the future. Take China. The country's population may stabilize at around 1.5 billion people sometime in the 2030s, but those with the eyes to see suspect that China will grow old before it grows rich. Worse, because of the way its one-child policy has favored the birth of boys, the country will be short of 30 million brides within fifteen years. The social, economic, and environmental implications are likely to be profound, and the efforts of people like social entrepreneur Wu Qing (discussed further in chapter 3), who founded the Beijing Cultural Development Center for Rural Women to help raise the status and expectations of rural Chinese women, will be central.

Many social entrepreneurs are focusing their efforts where the bulk of the world's population will be by the 2030s: the swarming megacities. Every year, some 70 million people leave their rural homes and migrate to cities. It is estimated that, by 2030, there will be some 2 billion squatters in the world—most living in what Robert Neuwirth has called "shadow cities," or megaslums.[11] These people are busily building a huge hidden economy. "Squatters are the largest builders of housing in the world," says Neuwirth, "and they are creating the cities of tomorrow." Anyone looking for clues about how a world of 7 billion to 10 billion people might be made survivable, let alone sustainable, ought to focus on—and support— social entrepreneurs, including such people as Tasneem Siddiqui in Pakistan, Sheela Patel and Jockin Arputham in India, and Taffy Adler in South Africa.[12]

They're Unreasonable Because They Seek Profit in Unprofitable Pursuits

Many of these entrepreneurs work in areas where there is partial or total market failure, which typically means that it is impossible to make the sort of money people expect to make in other areas of the economy. That doesn't mean, however, that social entrepreneurs are not interested in money. They, too, have families to support and bills to pay. What distinguishes them is that they are prepared to strike a very different balance when it comes to creating value for those who would not normally be able to afford it. It's interesting to note that a number of the better-known social entrepreneurs originally came from top consulting firms, so they chose to forfeit their high salaries to pursue other paths.

Social entrepreneurs frequently say that they have more than one bottom line—often two and, in some cases, three or four. As a result, their calculus is very different from that practiced in the mainstream, but the results are very clear in the progress they report.

Think of Ashok Khosla and Development Alternatives in India, which has been estimated to have created no less than half a million sustainable livelihoods. Think, too, of the Grameen Bank, which has helped some 7 million people (97 percent of them women), or of Grameenphone, with more than 10 million subscribers (three hundred thousand of them the so-called "telephone ladies," who rent out phones to other women). Or think of Riders for Health, which conservatively estimates that it is now helping provide some 11 million people with regular, reliable health care in otherwise inaccessible parts of Africa. That's world-class performance, however it may be measured.

Taking these people as a community, it is clear that a spectrum of innovation and enterprise is at work. At one end are those who struggle with absolute market failure, as in the poorest of the world's megaslums. Then, further along, there are those who are in the process of nurturing early-stage markets, like Waste Concern in Bangladesh, a prototype of a hybrid enterprise, as explained in chapter 1. Waste Concern has a nonprofit arm that focuses on pilot projects in areas like clean energy and recycling, while its for-profit arms focus on such areas as sustainable energy, waste projects, and consulting. And then, further along still, as in the burgeoning cleantech sector in the United States and the European Union, there are start-ups targeting new market needs. Here, the world of finance— of capital—is often impatient to get involved, because there are plenty of people willing and able to pay for new products and services. In fact, one reason that hybrid enterprises like Waste Concern are so interesting is that they can morph back and forth across that spectrum of opportunity and funding as the need dictates. Therein lies much of their power to tackle problems that others see as insoluble.

Those who back these organizations financially focus on investment, not charity. They are results oriented and bring business thinking to social value creation. Stephan Schmidheiny, the Swiss entrepreneur who made millions and set up a number of social investment initiatives, including Avina, makes it very clear that he is not in the charity game. "Probably the term *invest* best reflects our changed paradigm," he says. "Traditional foundations make do-nations. They grant money to finance a given project and expect reports on how that money has been spent. As a rule, little is done to evaluate the results achieved. Has anything changed? Has any-thing improved? If so, what and how? 'To invest' implies that we expect some sort of return, essentially high dividends for society and the environment. It also implies that we expect to be able to help determine the nature of that return."[13]

Two other groups with a growing interest in such entrepreneurs are corporate and private equity companies. For example, twenty-nine of the world's biggest private equity firms came together to create the pan-European Private Equity Foundation to focus on the underprivileged. Well-known organizations such as leveraged buyout firm Kohlberg Kravis Roberts & Co. (model for the novel *Barbarians at the Gate*), Blackstone, and Bain Capital were found-ing members.

Dig deep, and it is clear that social and environmental entre-preneurs are a good deal more reasonable than a cursory glance might suggest. For one thing, they are significantly more interested in working with mainstream business partners than most non-governmental organizations.[14] Muhammad Yunus, for example, has evolved into a serial entrepreneur, although many of his enter-prises have been built within the Grameen Group. His microcredit model has mutated to drive a range of new businesses, including Grameenphone (in partnership with Norway's Telenor) and Gra-meen Shakti, which offers solar energy solutions.[15] "The future of the world lies in the hands of market-based social entrepreneurs," he says. "The more we can move in the direction of business, the better off we are—in the sense that we are free. We have unlimited opportunities to expand and do more, and replication becomes so much easier. We can create a powerful alternative to the orthodoxy of capitalism—a social-consciousness-driven private sector, cre-ated by social entrepreneurs."[16]

While Yunus can picture mainstream business approaches being applied to social enterprise, in what he calls "social business en-trepreneurship," he envisions that investors in such enterprises "will invest for a return much broader than . . . immediate gain in dollars and cents."[17] Often, such investors are not interested in making private gains. For example, Grameen has linked up with the French food group Danone to form Grameen Danone Foods, where the bottom line "will be to deliver benefits to people and the planet, rather than to earn money for investors."[18]

However, the venture is turning out to have a significant impact on Danone's bottom line as well, according to CEO Frank Riboud, who sealed the deal with Yunus. Riboud describes how Danone's engineers have had to come up with different packaging strategies, to take account of Grameen's insistence on biodegradable containers—a modification that turns out to be attractive to the traditional environmentally conscious Danone consumer. In addition, Danone has had to rethink some aspects of its production, including the requirements of a completely new consumer who is much less likely to refrigerate the yogurt, eating it on the spot or shortly after purchase.

They're Unreasonable Because They Ignore the Evidence

Given that today's market research can so often be blind to tomorrow's looming risks and opportunities, it's not surprising that entrepreneurs ignore the evidence. Recall what the Body Shop International's Anita Roddick once said: market research is like looking in a rearview mirror. Or, as Bill Gates is supposed to have said: by the time there is a business case for action, it's likely too late. That's the way many social and environmental entrepreneurs feel, not because the markets are moving so rapidly, as they are for Microsoft, but because the relevant needs are so urgent. Such people typically act with urgency because it feels like the right thing to do, rather than because the research says that they stand to gain market share and make a great deal of money.

Clearly, if capital is to be well invested, market research and intelligence are critical. Indeed, most social entrepreneurs are very happy to take intelligence wherever they can find it, even if they cannot pay for it. Their success to date suggests that there are potentially huge new markets for the taking. Already, major companies, like Mexican cement maker Cemex, are finding that new business models can significantly extend the reach of products and services into communities that should be unable to pay for them and, in the process, create totally new markets.

Even if these entrepreneurs don't commission much in the way of research, intelligence on future needs flows in continuously. Take China, where Pan Yue, deputy director of the State Environmental Protection Agency, and his colleagues have been experimenting with new green gross domestic product (GDP) techniques. When they released the country's first green GDP report, after much number crunching, they noted with dismay that environment-related economic losses from absenteeism, illness, and death had already reached some $200 billion a year—or a tenth of the annual GDP.[19] By some measures, Pan told us, environmental losses are wiping out all the value of the giant country's annual economic growth. Although that information was not the result of market research, it signals powerful drivers of tomorrow's markets and huge growth opportunities for future innovators and entrepreneurs.

They're Unreasonable Because They Try to Measure the Unmeasurable

These entrepreneurs aim to provide forms of value that mainstream markets currently fail to recognize and reward. They know enough about business and markets to acknowledge that what gets measured is more likely to get funded, managed, and done. This takes them into a blizzard of acronyms: among them, DBL ("We have two bottom lines," declares social enterprise Rubicon, which embraces a double bottom line); TBL (add another—often, the environment—to get the triple bottom line); SROI (social return on investment); and BVP (the blended value proposition). "Communication is built on an understanding of a common language," as a leading guide on SROI put it, and "SROI is a particular language for communicating social, economic and environmental value."[20] This emerging discipline, which focuses on the measurement and valuation of nonfinancial or extrafinancial returns on investment, is complex, jargon riddled, and yet one of the most critical areas of research today.

Heavyweight actors are getting involved. Blended value pioneer Jed Emerson, for example, took a lead role in producing a survey of the related investment landscape for the World Economic Forum.[21] This survey explored some of the ways in which SROI and blended value thinking can inform debt finance, credit guarantees and enhancements, and private equity financing. One of the most interesting aspects of the project was its commentary on how "push" is giving way to "pull" in blended value investing.

Several decades ago, when hundreds of millions of dollars found their way into the emerging area of microfinance, funding was provided with little or no expectation of financial return. Over time, however, this push strategy has given way to more of a pull world, where risk capital is drawn into deals—in part, at least—by a desire for various types of return. For this to work and scale effectively, social entrepreneurs need to get much better at identifying, measuring, and pricing the social and environmental value they create.

Greg Dees of Duke University has argued that "markets do not do a good job of valuing social improvements, public goods and harms, and benefits for people who cannot afford to pay. These elements are often essential for social entrepreneurship."[22] By bringing natural, social, human, intellectual, and cultural forms of capital into the equation, social entrepreneurs aim to deliver real wealth to billions of people around the world who have so far been excluded from the benefits of the market economy. At the same time, however, these entrepreneurs are more interested in the long-term sustainability of their solutions than are most of their mainstream counterparts, and some plan to use the power of the business models they have developed on the fringes of today's economic system to invade and transform that system.

They're Unreasonable Because They Are Unqualified

It all depends on how you define *qualified*. Many of them are highly educated as engineers, medical doctors, lawyers, educators, public health specialists, journalists, and agricultural scientists, to name a few of the more heavily represented professions. But such credentials are altogether different from being qualified to advance massive social change. In fact, being locked into a discipline may be the wrong way to spark social innovation, which frequently entails combining multiple approaches and disciplines. Most social entrepreneurs stumble across the opportunity to serve others. Many of these people entered fields that they were not particularly well qualified for and worked out how to do things along the way. Rarely, if ever, did the answers to the problems come in a single blinding flash; by nature, the new areas of entrepreneurship are ill defined, explored, and understood.

This cuts countercurrent with much of contemporary education, particularly in the business world. "Young people should focus on building their career and making money," insisted one well-known panelist at an event organized by the World Economic Forum. "Once they have made their money, then they can think about becoming social entrepreneurs," he asserted. The social entrepreneurs sitting in the audience exchanged uncomfortable glances. Their unease with the panelist's comment was summed up by Linda Rottenberg, a visionary social entrepreneur and the cofounder and CEO of Endeavor, who was on the same panel. "The idea that a social entrepreneur should wait until the time and the finances are right to launch their venture is nonsense," she retorted. "Being a social entrepreneur is not really a career choice. We can't help being the way we are. We are born this way."[23]

If social entrepreneurs are born, not made, why are the world's leading graduate schools of business—home of the MBA and birthplace of the business plan—rushing to set up courses and programs on social entrepreneurship for their students? Because many of the key skills have wider applications in the private, public, and citizen sectors. (The term *citizen sector*, coined by Ashoka, aims to avoid the negative associations of the *non-* in nonprofit and non-governmental, for example.[24])

Listen to Bo Peabody, a highly successful serial entrepreneur who sold his first venture at age twenty-one for $60 million and has gone on to spin off multiple other successful ventures. "When I was growing up, 'entrepreneur' carried roughly the same connotation as 'inventor,'" he recalls. "The word conjured up images of your wacky uncle doing science experiments in his basement in search of a new species of peanut butter. But by the late nineties, 'entrepreneur' meant millionaire and celebrity. And that meant everyone wanted to be an entrepreneur. The problem is this: Very few people *are* entrepreneurs." Peabody goes on to say, "People often ask me, 'When did you decide to become an entrepreneur?' I never decided to be an entrepreneur. It just happened. I started mowing lawns when I was ten. I moved to snow-blowing the driveways next to those lawns when I was thirteen. And finally on to seal-coating those same driveways when I was sixteen. My logic: I had customers, and the more distasteful, dirty and degrading a task it was to maintain a square foot of their property, the more they were willing to pay me to do it. Pretty simple."[25]

The central point Peabody makes is this: "Entrepreneurs are born, not made. One does not decide to be an entrepreneur. One *is* an entrepreneur. Those who decide to become entrepreneurs are making the first in a long line of bad business decisions."[26] Born entrepreneurs, Peabody notes, tend to have short attention spans. Managers, by contrast, can stay focused on one thing for longer. Entrepreneurs think laterally, but managers are more prone to think in a linear manner. Ultimately, it is a question of where you are in the business life cycle. The start-up phase of any enterprise necessitates flexibility and quick responses, which the entrepreneur does best. As the venture matures and grows, linear thought is fundamental—and that is what the MBA prepares students to do. So, although most MBA programs are unlikely to be key spawning grounds for entrepreneurs, the current increase of graduate courses in social innovation and entrepreneurship is still an encouraging trend, given the need for a wide array of managers and financial and marketing experts to strengthen this growing sector.

*They're Unreasonable Because They
Refuse to Be Made into Superheroes*

Any group of entrepreneurs, business or otherwise, will have its share of egomaniacs, but the social entrepreneurs we have met and worked with to date seem strongly skewed to the good-fun-to-be-around end of the spectrum. They do not seem to be burdened with Napoleon or Superman complexes, or anything like that. Indeed, one of their most striking characteristics is their ready admission that the challenges they relish are way beyond any single entrepreneur or enterprise.

While these entrepreneurs will not be able to secure the future alone, their thinking, strategies, business models, and ways of measuring multiple dimensions of value have a great deal to offer and teach the rest of us. Their life stories also have much to teach us all about the nature of tomorrow's challenges—and about the market strategies and business models that are likely to help tackle those challenges.

"We have no super-hero," said Sir Richard Branson when launching his $25 million Virgin Earth Challenge in 2007. "We have only our own ingenuity to fall back on." [27] He was inspired to launch that contest by past examples like the Ansari X Prize, which resulted in the first private manned space flight in 2004, and the eighteenth-century challenge that spurred the pursuit for a device that would measure longitude. Branson is looking for a commercially viable technology that will result in "the net removal of anthropogenic, atmospheric greenhouse gases each year for at least 10 years without countervailing harmful effects." And, a condition that could keep Branson's money in the bank for a while, the technology has to remove at least 1 billion metric tons of carbon dioxide from the atmosphere each year. There's ambition for you.

The X Prize Foundation has already announced its second major challenge—the Archon X Prize for Genomics—and has been working on others in the social domain, including contests designed to spur innovative thinking about cars, health care, and poverty.[28] But even if it achieves its aim of awarding $200 million or more in ten to fifteen new prize categories over the next five years, there is a bigger challenge still. Funding gaps remain central to the question of whether anything like global sustainability will be achieved during this century, an issue to which we will return later.

They're Unreasonable Because They Are, Well, Unreasonable

It almost goes without saying that the sort of people who want to shake things up, to change things, can get under other people's skins. It goes with the territory, the breed, the trade. And it is one of the factors that can lead to the ejection of the founding entrepreneur—or entrepreneurs—from an enterprise. Anyone charged with ensuring good governance in fast-evolving social and environmental enterprises needs to remember that highly charged entrepreneurs can break a lot of eggs while making their omelets. Their impatience can make them tough to work with, even when there are not more fundamental problems, like the sexual harassment allegations that led to the resignation of the founder of Habitat for Humanity, to tackle.

Some of these entrepreneurs certainly live life on the edge, in multiple dimensions. Take Dov Charney, the wildly unconventional and controversial chief executive of American Apparel—and a self-confessed sex addict.[29] That is something you can find in many sectors of the economy and of wider society, of course, though in these media-driven times the related behaviors can introduce additional risks to already risky ventures.

Charney, nonetheless, has presided over one of the fastest-growing companies in the clothing sector, and American Apparel has made ethical treatment of its employees a major feature of its company policies at a time when most of its competitors have been involved in a race to the bottom with cheap Chinese imports. At least 20 percent of the fabric used at Charney's American Apparel is organic, with plans to push that proportion toward 80 percent; the company recycles its fabric scraps; and the factory has a solar roof. To fund the scaling of the business, Charney sold American Apparel to a publicly listed shell company, Endeavor Acquisition, for $384.5 million.[30] But there are potential problems in this seemingly unstoppable formula. One journalist who experienced the sexual mayhem that surrounds Charney describes him as "a madman" but added, "I like that."[31] On the other hand, it is at least conceivable that others will eventually decide otherwise, concluding that such behavior betrays the ethical code people like Ashoka's Bill Drayton lay such store by.

The Structure of This Book

We've divided the chapters that follow into three sections, each one full of issues and examples from the world of social and environmental entrepreneurs.

Part I focuses on how unreasonable entrepreneurs build their enterprises—and on some of the challenges they face along the way. Part II investigates the implications of their work for future market risks and opportunities. Part III lays out some of the lessons that leaders and decision makers in the private, public, and citizen sectors can learn from the progress these people have made to date and highlights some actions they will need to take if the current momentum is to be maintained or even accelerated.

Our conclusion draws out some lessons for mainstream businesses and leaders from other key institutions and offers a series of recommendations—from the entrepreneurs themselves—about the many ways we can all support their work.

Throughout this book you will meet scores of entrepreneurs whose experiences will inform the most important choices for the future. We hope you will find their stories as compelling, provocative, ingenious, and inspiring as we do.

Part I

Building Innovative Enterprises

ONE

Creating Successful Business Models

I T IS IN THE NATURE of their work at the bleeding edge of change that social and environmental entrepreneurs are often seen to be unreasonable; the successful organizations they build, however, are anything but. Of course, people say that anyone could have predicted that a Grameen Bank or a Green Belt Movement would work, but very few people foresaw the longer-term success of Amazon, eBay, or Google. Whether entrepreneurs plan out their futures in great detail or rely on trial and error, these world-changing pioneers are learning to channel their irrepressible convictions, their boundless creativity, and their ability to amass the necessary resources into building sustainable systems and structures that address the most pressing market failures of our time.

Inevitably, many start out by responding to natural disasters (like earthquakes, hurricanes, tsunamis, famine, disease) or man-made ones (like war). The twenty-first century is likely to produce as many—if not more of—such out-of-the-blue stimuli to action. But this isn't just about responding to existing catastrophes. Many environmental entrepreneurs, for example, are galvanized by the prospect of global climate change or other human-induced insults to the natural world. All seem driven by deeply personal, emotional responses to a disaster (or a sense of impending disaster) that threatens vast populations or ecological treasures both big and small.

Stand back, however, and it is clear that current emergency response activities and the strategies that evolve from them can rarely be called "sustainable." No matter how innovative and effective these efforts may be, they are still largely band-aid solutions. Nevertheless, a significant number of social entrepreneurs who began their work in response to specific emergencies have evolved their interventions into sustainable, transformational solutions that help prevent further disasters—or, at least, ensure coordinated and effective responses.

Some of the resulting nonprofit ventures have grown into globally respected organizations, notably Henri Dunant's Red Cross and Bernard Kouchner's Médecins Sans Frontières. Among the examples profiled in these pages, Fazle Abed's BRAC in Bangladesh and Joe Madiath's Gram Vikas in India come to mind, as do Andrea and Barry Coleman's Riders for Health in Africa, Jeroo Billimoria's Child Helpline International (which started in India and then went global), and Ibrahim Abouleish's Sekem in Egypt.

One central goal for such social enterprises—and for those who fund them—is leverage. We use this term not necessarily in the narrow accounting sense of financial leverage, although securing adequate financial resources is a critical concern for these organizations. Rather, it means leveraging all kinds of resources—from indigenous capabilities and social capital to philanthropic and governmental support, business partnerships, and income from previously untapped markets.

Increasingly, small groups of people use multiple kinds of leverage to drive change on a disproportionate scale.[1] As a result, they are able to transform their ventures and, in some cases, the entire system of which they are a part. Their efforts create new markets and new levels of influence, often outpacing established nongovernmental organizations and mainstream business organizations.

Our best social and environmental entrepreneurs tend to excel no matter what organizational principles they adopt, but each typical structure has both advantages and drawbacks in different situations. So—like scientists racing to unlock secrets of the human genome—venture philanthropists, foundations, government agencies, and businesses are trying to uncover these entrepreneurs' secrets to success. And just as the human genome is constructed from a small number of building blocks, so too leading social enterprises seem to be built from a relatively small number of key ingredients.

The resulting structures tend to fall into three categories, or business models, which we call the "leveraged nonprofit" (model 1), the "hybrid nonprofit" (model 2), and the "social business" (model 3). All pursue social or environmental ends that the markets have largely or totally failed to address, and they use different means to do so. In the process, they may adopt unique leadership, management, and fund-raising styles, each with its own implications and lessons for people working in mainstream organizations in the public, private, or civil society sectors.

Each model offers different challenges and opportunities for would-be partners and other entrepreneurs. In this chapter we examine each one in turn, exploring several compelling examples and describing the ways they have developed. We conclude by describing one social enterprise that has morphed into a fully capitalized and profitable mainstream business without losing sight of its original goal.

Model 1: Leveraged Nonprofit Ventures

Many kinds of market failure are difficult—if not impossible—to tackle using for-profit business models. In such areas nonprofit models are likely to be the only option. The key is to leverage available resources in ways that measure up to the nature and scale of the challenges and to do so when the immediate crises that typically drive emergency responses have faded or have yet to materialize. But nonprofits can be much harder to scale than for-profit ventures. According to the Bridgespan Group, of the 200,000 nonprofits started in the United States since 1970, only 144 have reached $50 million in annual revenue.[2]

Until recently, many people assumed that social entrepreneurs acted in the nonprofit world because their funding mainly came from the government or foundations. This has been particularly the case in the United States, where the substantial incentives for various forms of charitable giving include clear tax benefits. The paradox is that in the process, nonprofit enterprises have become uncomfortably—and often unproductively—dependent on philanthropic largesse and all the exemptions that accrue to entities operating in the public interest. This dependence generally runs counter to the possibility of expansion. In an increasingly competitive environment, the number of nonprofit organizations seeking funding has rapidly outpaced the supply of donor dollars, while the adequacy and availability of specifically targeted expansion capital has become even more problematic.

Ask most model 1 entrepreneurs why they are not working on a for-profit basis, however, and they will look at you as if you are from another planet. These people aim to meet needs that are ignored by current market mechanisms and businesses. Maybe this blinds them to the occasional opportunity to operate on a for-profit basis, but generally they operate where the market air is too thin for mainstream businesses to even think of venturing.

Model 1 entrepreneurship tends to distinguish sharply between private and public goods. *Private goods* are ones people can own individually and are typically produced by for-profit businesses. In contrast, a *public good* is one where the consumption of the good by one individual does not reduce the amount available for consumption by others.[3] So if an individual eats a cake, there is no cake left for anyone else; if an individual breathes air or drinks water from a stream, there is still air or water available to others.

Although governments are often involved in producing and ensuring access to public goods, they are not always the only ones;

many private firms are involved in so doing, as is the case with health, education, safe drinking water, housing, and the like. Entrepreneurs step in to fill the gap where governments are not able—or willing—to provide a public good and where the private sector cannot justify the risk in relation to the rewards.

The following characteristics are typical of most model 1 enterprises:

- A public good is being delivered to the most economically vulnerable, who do not have access to, or are unable to afford, the service rendered.

- Both the entrepreneur and the organization are change catalysts, with a central goal of enabling direct beneficiaries to assume ownership of the initiative, enhancing its longer-term sustainability.

- Multiple external partners are actively involved in supporting (or are being recruited to support) the venture financially, politically, and in kind.

- The founding entrepreneur morphs into a figurehead, in some cases for the wider movement, as others assume responsibilities and leadership.

You could argue that entrepreneurs applying leveraged non-profit approaches are modern-day alchemists who, with minimal financing, leverage the power of communities to transform an otherwise grim daily existence. And, while they learn a good deal from their failures, the best of them are proving more successful than the alchemists, whose experiments heralded the dawn of the industrial era—laying the foundations on which "real" science would later be built. In like manner, leading social entrepreneurs signal where the coming years will head. But companies—and other potential mainstream partners—should not be fooled into thinking that these entrepreneurs' dependence on external funds and in-kind support will make them easy partners. Quite the contrary. Many carry an understandable rage born from years of watching their communities being shortchanged, ignored, or destroyed by greed. That said, mainstream businesses that create successful partnerships with these enterprises will likely find their thinking challenged, their horizons stretched, and their own employees reinvigorated.

It is no accident that much early model 1 entrepreneurship evolved in the context of strong religious convictions, as was the case of Mother Teresa and Habitat for Humanity. Others, like Barefoot College, which we examine next, grew out of a justified sense of rage with a system that locks people into generations of poverty and exclusion.

Bunker Roy and Barefoot College

Let's start with Barefoot College, a prototypical model 1 enterprise whose founder, Bunker Roy, might seem the quintessence of unreasonableness. Roy was born to the Indian elite, was educated in India's leading public schools (i.e., nongovernmental schools, the equivalent of private schools in the United States), and even represented India in the squash world championships, for which he is still celebrated by squash aficionados. You might say he had it made, but he turned his back on it all, eschewing the trappings of privilege, and founded Barefoot College, an Indian organization that has had a huge impact in defining and driving what Roy calls the "barefoot" approach to development.

This approach rests on the idea that anyone can become anything—from an architect to a solar engineer—without formal education. So Barefoot College set out to leverage local skills and capabilities. For more than thirty years, Roy's work has made him a leading figure in the Indian civil society sector, frequently upsetting—generally to his infinite amusement—the powers that be and, in the process, inspiring many younger activists and social entrepreneurs.

Evolving out of the Social Work and Research Centre, Barefoot College was created in 1972 by a group of students from top Indian universities under Roy's leadership. Based in Tilonia, Rajasthan, it was built around the Gandhian concept of the village as a self-reliant unit. By applying traditional but informal educational processes to manage, control, and own technologies designed to meet basic needs, the college helps illiterate or semiliterate poor people in rural areas learn to use these technologies without relying on outside paper-qualified experts. All staff at the college take a living wage, not a market wage—and the maximum living wage is $100 a month.

The central principle is simple. To improve their quality of life, Roy stresses, the rural poor must be able to satisfy their basic needs, like drinking water, health, education, and employment. Billions of dollars are spent every year to provide these services from the top. Colleges, research institutes, and funding organizations employ urban-trained, paper-qualified professionals to provide these services at tremendous cost, but the Barefoot College team argues that in such cases there will always be a vested interest in applying a top-down approach.

Poverty today is big business, Roy argues: in effect, many mainstream players want to keep the rural population poor because thousands of urban jobs are at stake. By contrast, the Barefoot College thesis is that development programs do not need urban-based professionals because paraprofessionals already exist in the villages, and their wisdom, traditional knowledge, and practical down-to-earth skills are not identified, mobilized, or applied—indeed, such people are generally penalized because they do not have a formal educational qualification.

Barefoot College provides abundant evidence of the capacity of ordinary people to identify, analyze, and solve their own problems. Over the years, it has trained barefoot doctors, teachers, engineers, architects, designers, metal workers, IT specialists, and communicators. And the results speak for themselves. This is the only college based in a rural area that is built by the poor and managed by them. Barefoot engineers have solar-electrified the college: indeed, it is still the only fully solar-electrified college in India. Barefoot solar engineers, many of them illiterate women, have solar-electrified thousands of houses in eight Indian states. Barefoot water engineers installed the first hand pumps ever in Ladakh, fourteen thousand feet up in the Himalayas, something that urban experts had said was technically impossible.

One of the most unusual aspects of the informal education the college provides is the night schools for children whose various responsibilities keep them from attending school in the morning. Over three thousand boys and girls attend 150 night schools. One unique aspect of their education is the emphasis on governance: the management, supervision, and administration of these schools are in the hands of a children's parliament. Every three years, the children elect a prime minister and a cabinet of ministers, who are between six and fourteen years old. (All three of the prime ministers elected to date have been girls.) The present prime minister looks after twenty goats in the morning but is prime minister in the evening. In the same spirit of democracy and transparency, Barefoot College was the first—and remains one of the few—community-based organizations in India to have conducted a social audit, opening all its accounts to public scrutiny and answering questions from the community in a public hearing.

Meanwhile, traditional barefoot communicators using puppets have changed the attitudes of many communities on issues such as child marriage, the rights of women, equal wages for women, and legal literacy. And Roy loses few opportunities when speaking overseas to tell audiences that the puppets were made from papier-mâché produced by recycling World Bank reports. True or not, the story sticks in the audience's memory and, with it, the fundamental principle of people taking their destinies into their own hands.

A visit to Barefoot College redefines the concept of simple living, as one young Australian engineer put it. While the college is life transforming for all those involved, without Roy's enormous capacity to raise external resources, it would be difficult to keep pace with some of Barefoot's current projects, including hosting solar engineers in training from other countries. This is particularly important because the college's efforts have catalyzed generation upon generation of trainees who return to their rural communities in developing countries with the knowledge and skills needed to construct rainwater-harvesting tanks from local materials or to solar-electrify their villages and others. Comparing typical costs to the expenditures made through international aid and international consultants, Barefoot College's solutions look like an amazing bargain.

When we asked Bunker Roy what governments and mainstream business can learn from the Barefoot College experience, he replied, "First unlearn and then relearn from the simple examples of the rural poor and their amazing capacity and competence to think of simple barefoot solutions. They said of Mahatma Gandhi how expensive it was to make him look simple! Today, regrettably, this is what could be said of governments and mainstream business."[4] If there is one lesson that emerges from the Barefoot College story, it is an age-old one: visionary, energetic, and inclusive leaders can release extraordinary human potential.

Model 2: Hybrid Nonprofit Ventures

Innovation happens in each of the three models, but the most experimentation happens with hybrid nonprofit business models. Many of the new philanthropists strongly favor model 2 enterprises and are eager to work with them. One key reason: these people hope (even expect) that such organizations' imaginative blending of nonprofit and revenue-generating for-profit strategies will produce unexpected forms of hybrid vigor. Also, the more businesslike aspects of a hybrid venture can make it seem more normal than a model 1 venture, where there is no realistic prospect of profit, either now or—in some cases—ever.

As in biological hybridization, the process of creating entrepreneurial hybrids can be time consuming, the results uncertain, and the opportunity costs fairly high. Whereas biology's so-called F1 hybrids can display significantly improved growth and yield, model 2 ventures have the potential to reach new levels of social or environmental value creation.[5]

Hybrid enterprises model some of the novel forms of social and environmental value creation that will be central to business success and sustainability in the coming decades. Their main characteristics include the following:

- As with model 1 ventures, goods and/or services are delivered to populations that have been excluded or underserved by mainstream markets, but the notion of making (and reinvesting) a profit is not totally out of the question.

- Sooner or later, the founding entrepreneur—or his or her team—typically develops a marketing plan to ensure that the poor or otherwise disadvantaged can access the product or service being provided.

- The enterprise is able to recover a portion of its costs through the sale of goods and services, in the process often identifying new markets.

- To sustain activities and address the unmet needs of poor or otherwise marginalized clients, the entrepreneur mobilizes funds from public, private, and/or philanthropic organizations in the form of grants, loans, or, in rarer cases, quasi-equity investments.

- As mainstream investors and businesses enter the picture, even when they are not seeking mainstream financial returns, they tend to push hybrid nonprofit ventures to become model 3 social businesses, to ensure access to new sources of funding, particularly capital markets. This may be warranted in some cases, but it risks refocusing activities to the point where the poorest will no longer be served.

Let's take as our examples here a pair of hybrid ventures: Rubicon in the United States, which creates jobs for the disadvantaged, and Aravind in India, which restores eyesight to those unable to pay for the necessary operations.

Rick Aubry and Rubicon Programs

The first of our model 2 hybrids was founded as a nonprofit organization in 1973, but it was not until 1986, when entrepreneur Rick Aubry took over, that Rubicon Programs became a recognized leader in the social enterprise world. Rubicon was the first multiservice agency in the United States to link a real job with decent housing and a support system to sustain homeless or otherwise disadvantaged people who are trying to make positive changes in their lives.

Rubicon's business ventures were originally conceived to provide training opportunities for poor clients. But the businesses were approaching a scale where their own needs and the needs of the training programs were no longer aligned. So in 1986, when Aubry took over, he and his colleagues asked themselves a question: was the primary strategy to offer training opportunities, or was it to run successful businesses that could create jobs and sustain a training component? If the answer was the former, Rubicon would always be 100 percent donor dependent—a pure model 1 nonprofit. If the answer was the latter, Rubicon could offer training *and* earn an income from the services provided (and thereby empower people by allowing them to be part of a successful enterprise in the mainstream market). As a result of these deliberations, Rubicon took the second approach, deciding that each of its businesses would have to succeed in the competitive market in which it operated, a model that others now emulate.

Under Aubry's leadership, Rubicon has incorporated mainstream business principles into its practice and built two highly successful social enterprises: Rubicon Landscape Services, which generates annual revenues of more than $4 million, and Rubicon Bakery, one of the San Francisco Bay Area's leading bakeries, with annual sales of $2 million. Employees are primarily people with little or no work history who are trying to overcome the challenges of poverty, homelessness, and/or mental health disabilities. By contrast, the customers of Rubicon's high-end baked goods and its high-quality landscaping services are well to do. A fundamental lesson that Rubicon has learned is that while people may like its social mission, they tend to base their buying decisions on the quality and value of Rubicon's products and services.

If you ask Rick Aubry what governments and mainstream businesses can learn from the Rubicon experience, he replies, "We focus on the outcomes that people want. The people we serve want a decent job, a place to live, and to be part of the community. By focusing on creating jobs in our businesses and with our partners and building a comprehensive range of services to make sure that people succeed in their own lives, we have created a model that governments can emulate—and that businesses can support."[6]

Dr. Venkataswamy and the Aravind Eye Care System

The Aravind Eye Care System offers one of the most intriguing hybrid models. Founded over thirty years ago by the late Dr. Venkataswamy (or "Dr. V.") and based in India, it has potentially huge implications for the health-care business worldwide, with the model even proving viable in the United States. Dr. V. and his team turned an eleven-bed eye clinic into one of the largest and most productive eye-care facilities in the world. The Aravind community has been unreasonable in exactly the same way Gandhi was—refusing to accept that the future would be a straight-line extension of current reality.

Taking its services to the doorstep of rural India, the Aravind Eye Care System has become self-sustaining—treating over 2 million patients a year (two-thirds of them for free or with a steep subsidy) and still managing to make a profit that it reinvests in growing the enterprise and continuously upgrading its services. It is an international resource and training center that is revolutionizing hundreds of eye care programs in developing countries. Amazingly, with less than 1 percent of the country's ophthalmic workforce, Aravind performs about 5 percent of all cataract surgeries in India. Since its inception, Aravind has performed more than 2.8 million surgeries and handled over 22 million outpatients.

Aravind has pioneered a sustainable model that follows the principle that large-volume, high-quality, and community-centric services can result in low-cost and long-term viability. By charging wealthier patients more and poorer patients less, it has developed a sustainable business model. This success has been achieved without diluting poor patients' quality of care. As a result of the unique fee system and effective management, Aravind is able to provide free eye care to the majority of its patients.

To give some sense of the potential of this approach, there are an estimated 37 million people worldwide who are blind and an additional 124 million who are visually impaired. The global economic burden of blindness is estimated to be around $25 billion per year. Almost 90 percent of the blind live in developing countries that face the challenges of a growing population, inadequate infrastructure, low per capita income, illiteracy, and diseases in epidemic proportions. In India alone, an estimated 12 million are blind, yet 60 percent of blindness there is a result of cataracts, which are almost always curable.

A key part of the challenge has been getting health care to those in need. So, for example, 70 percent of India's 1 billion people live in rural areas. By contrast, 80 percent of the ten thousand ophthalmic surgeons in the country live in urban areas. Given the magnitude of the blindness problem, the government alone cannot meet the needs of all at risk. Realizing this, in what looks like a modern miracle even at close quarters, Dr. V. established an alternate health-care model that would both supplement the efforts of the government and be self-supporting.

Ask Thulsi Ravilla, Dr. V.'s successor as executive director, what others can learn from the Aravind experience, and he advises:

> When trying to reach economically poor sections of the population or engaging in development work, you have to transcend the stage where you are simply reacting to market demands, shifting instead to "market driving." In most such situations, while the need or potential may exist, the market doesn't. The market-driving approach potentially gives invaluable insight

into the design and development of products or services, their pricing, and [their] delivery mechanisms. This approach essentially defines the design parameters for success. When you look back at developmental initiatives that have failed or succeeded, you see this common thread, and this applies equally to government programs and business activities.[7]

The motivation for exploring so-called base-of-the-pyramid markets may be to address government or market failures and bring much-needed benefits to poor people or, in the case of the more commercially minded, to make money in unlikely circumstances. Just as important as the immediate questions about who will benefit and who will profit from such ventures is what they tell us about the nature and scale of the nascent markets they serve. Because they operate in emerging markets, model 1 and 2 initiatives may provide early indications of where business could head in the future. The potential for services, products, and technologies created at this level to leapfrog back into developed world markets can only grow.

Model 3: Social Business Ventures

Model 3 ventures, many of which first appeared outside the United States, may have evolved as an interesting but unintended by-product of the smaller philanthropic funds available to social entrepreneurs in other countries. Such limited resources forced entrepreneurs to set up their enterprises as social businesses—that is, for-profit entities focused on social missions. A survey of the 98 ventures formed by 115 social entrepreneurs from the Schwab Foundation's network of accomplished practitioners showed that just under one-third (30) headed model 3 social businesses. Only 2 of those enterprises, however, are based in the United States, despite the fact that the total number of U.S.-based entrepreneurs in the network is 20. The remaining 18 are model 1 leveraged nonprofit enterprises or model 2 nonprofit-based hybrids.

On the other hand, particularly in the United States, the for-profit social business is the model of choice for most environmental entrepreneurs—perhaps because there are already more obvious market opportunities for ecofriendly products and services.

Model 3 ventures are distinct from their model 1 and 2 counterparts. They are set up as for-profit businesses from the outset, though they tend to think about the question of what to do with any profits very differently than mainstream businesses. The main characteristics of people and enterprises operating in this zone include the following:

- The entrepreneur sets up the venture as a business with the specific mission to drive transformational social and/or environmental change.

- Profits are generated, but the main aim is not to maximize financial returns for shareholders but instead to financially benefit low-income groups and to grow the social venture by reinvestment, enabling it to reach and serve more people.

- The entrepreneur seeks out investors interested in combining financial and social returns.

- The enterprise's financing—and scaling—opportunities can be significantly greater because social businesses can more easily take on debt and equity.

Balancing such a venture's social mission and its financial sustainability can, however, create internal tensions. The founding entrepreneur must exercise a strong leadership role, which may make succession more challenging than it is with leveraged or hybrid organizations. On the plus side, social businesses are significantly easier for mainstream businesspeople to understand—and to develop partnerships with. This, in turn, facilitates (at least in principle) these organizations' access to capital markets, a window that's closed for philanthropy-dependent entrepreneurs.

To date, the best-known social businesses tend to be found in the area of microfinance, including the Grameen Bank and BRAC in Bangladesh, SKS Microfinance and Basix in India, and Acción and Finca in the United States. But the number of these organizations is growing, and—particularly in the area of cleantech—they are gaining traction. Let's look at two social businesses that are quite different from those described in the sections on model 1 and model 2 organizations, as well as from the microfinance institutions just mentioned.

Ibrahim Abouleish and Sekem

Our first example was founded by Dr. Ibrahim Abouleish. Sekem, headquartered outside Cairo, takes its name from the hieroglyphic transcription meaning "vitality of the sun" and was the first entity to develop biodynamic farming methods in Egypt. Similar in many ways to organic farming, this approach also utilizes astronomical principles for planting. The approach is built around the notion that profit making can go hand in hand with an integrated socio-economic business model, providing employees and farming communities throughout the country with the opportunity to improve their education, health, and quality of life.

Sekem's six businesses generate revenue and are grouped into a holding company that provides centralized services, including financial, quality assurance, information technology, and human resources. The first company, Isis, is a household brand in Egypt. It produces and packs bread, dairy products, oils, spices, teas, honey, jams, cereals, and many other food products that are sold in grocery stores and other shops throughout Egypt and abroad. The second, Atos Pharma, established in 1986 as a joint venture company with German companies, focuses on developing the Egyptian phytopharmaceuticals market (phytopharmaceuticals are drugs created from plant compounds—a higher-quality form of herbal medicines). This, according to Sekem's CFO, is Sekem's biggest income generator. A group of physicians and pharmacists work together in the research and development of new products for different conditions. One early indicator of quality: in 1992, Atos secured a license agreement with Weleda, a leading manufacturer of phytopharmaceuticals in Germany, to manufacture and market natural cosmetics in Egypt.

The third company, Libra, was set up by Sekem in 1988. It is a farming company that supplies raw materials to the other Sekem companies for further processing and production. It arranges long-term agreements with farmers, ensuring them favorable conditions independent of price fluctuations in domestic and global markets. We spoke to a number of farmers about why they stick with Sekem when the market price for their produce can sometimes be higher than Sekem's price, and their consistent response was security in the long term. Sekem has a participatory approach to setting product prices. Each year, farmers talk with wholesalers, retailers, and consumers to set an optimum price for their products. That price considers incurred costs and a margin that will allow the farmer to develop further. This transparent system based on information and feedback creates trust between Sekem and the farmers and frees farmers from the anxiety of finding a buyer that will give them a fraction more per unit. Farmers also note that the organic method provides them with consistently better yields per acre year after year than the chemical method.

Fourth is Hator, established in 1996, which produces and packs fresh fruit and vegetables for local and export markets. Internationally, the products are sold through Organic Farm Food in the United Kingdom and through Eosta in the Netherlands. Hator is the fastest-growing Sekem business, and it consistently meets the demand of European and local customers. Fifth are the Sekem shops, set up in 1996, which offer a complete range of Sekem products. Finally, there is Conytex, which processes cotton without any synthetic chemical additives, producing beautiful, high-quality children's and babies' wear. Partner companies export the clothes to buyers in the United States, Germany, Switzerland, and Austria. The clothing is marketed locally under the name Cotton People Organic. In Europe it is called Alnatura, and in the United States it is sold as Under the Nile.

Sekem's growth has been meteoric. It now employs two thousand people and has become a nationally renowned enterprise and a market leader in organic food products and phytopharmaceuticals. It has established links with European and American customers in the export trade, which account for 45 percent of its overall sales. Its commitment to innovative development led to the nation-wide application of organic methods to control pests and improve crop yields. In collaboration with Egypt's ministry of agriculture, for example, Sekem deployed a new system of plant protection for cotton, reducing a farm's total pesticide intake by more than 90 percent, which led to a ban on crop dusting all over Egypt.

Egypt's many social and environmental problems are interrelated and include overpopulation, environmental degradation, inadequate education, and health care. Agriculture involves around 40 percent of the workforce and remains the least developed sector of the economy. The cost of agricultural production has increased as the land and natural resource base has shrunk. As a result, Egypt has become one of the world's largest importers of food. Because of the interconnectedness of the country's problems, Sekem has integrated into its operations a thriving social and cultural dimension to help address Egypt's crumbling health, educational, and cultural-preservation capacities.

As Abouleish explains:

> The Sekem initiative was founded to realize the vision of sustainable human development. It aims to contribute to the comprehensive development of the individual, society, and the environment. A holistic concept encompassing integrated economic, social, and cultural development forms the key to the Sekem vision. The initiative is formed of three independent, but closely interrelated, entities. First, Sekem Holding, a group of companies, producing a wide range of goods for national and international markets, based on products from Sekem's own biodynamic [i.e., organic] agriculture. Second, the Cooperative of Sekem Employees, which seeks to develop work models that ensure respect for human dignity, safeguard human rights, and guarantee the equality of everybody in the community. And,

third, the Sekem Development Foundation, which is supported by the group companies and provides education, training, and health care for the local population, as well as [conducts] social and scientific research.[8]

When we asked Abouleish what governments and mainstream business can learn from Sekem, he suggested, "Governments and mainstream business can recognize and respect the three independent domains: culture, economy, and legal—and foster cooperation and interaction to foster human development."[9]

Cristóbal Colón and La Fageda

The second of our social businesses was founded by Christopher Columbus. No, not *that* one—but, yes, his name is really Cristóbal Colón ("the good one," as he likes to emphasize). A Spaniard, he started his career at age fourteen working for his uncle, a tailor, but possessed by a desire to work with the mentally ill, he studied psychiatry and later found himself working in a hospital for the insane. Work therapy was the treatment of choice at the time—this was the late 1970s—and Colón was put in charge of the relevant program. This entailed assigning useless tasks to the patients to keep them occupied, including making ceramic ashtrays, book marks, and other little trinkets like those a five-year-old brings home from art class or summer camp. There is no market for such items, and really only a mother could cherish them. Whereas most reasonable people would have accepted this approach as the way mentally ill people were treated, Colón grew frustrated with the patients' meaningless activity. They might be crazy, he thought, but they are not stupid; they need to feel worthwhile. Like Rick Aubry at Rubicon Programs, Colón realized that one thing that would provide a sense of purpose was a real job in a real company that produced something other people genuinely wanted to buy.

It was 1982 at the time, and living in Cataluña, Colón decided to set up a dairy business. But he needed capital, so he visited a bank to ask for a loan. Imagine being the loan officer in a bank where a psychiatrist shows up asking to borrow money. He says that his name is Christopher Columbus and that he wants to set up a dairy company that will employ mostly mentally ill workers. Now there is an unreasonable person, you might conclude, perhaps someone who is even verging on insanity himself.

Undeterred, Colón got his way. Today, La Fageda, his dairy farm, is a thriving business and has the third-largest market share for yogurt in Cataluña—outdone only by Danone and Nestlé. It still employs the mentally ill. Its annual revenue is over $10 million, and it is now fully self-sustaining. It pays its workers well, and they may choose to live on site, which many opt to do. La Fageda works closely with the public sector, which refers psychiatric patients to the company for training, employment at La Fageda, and eventual reincorporation into society, where possible. It has a fully staffed mental health facility on site, providing ongoing support for workers. It is certified by Spain's ministry of agriculture as a dairy farm, and most of its customers are completely unaware that the mentally ill are responsible for producing the products they enjoy. (Typically, people buy La Fageda's products because they taste great, not out of charity.) Meanwhile, the mentally ill are no longer viewed as "patients," which is a disempowering term; they earn their living by contributing to one of their country's leading dairy companies and are proud of that fact.

La Fageda—like Sekem—is a for-profit business, but not a profit-maximizing business. Its business is social transformation, and its profits are used as a means to that end. Working with the mentally ill is La Fageda's core business, not a public relations afterthought or part of the company's social responsibility activities. Although it provides a public health service by supporting the mentally ill—a task usually left to the government—it is not a government organization, and it is most certainly not a charity, which would make it dependent on donor funding and philanthropy.

Cristóbal Colón says this about what other sectors can learn from his experience: "La Fageda is a company that was constructed in reverse. Its first asset was the workers, a group that needed to be employed—ex-interns in the psychiatric hospital in Girona. Subsequently, the company was created. La Fageda demonstrates that a company that starts with people, putting people before profits, can grow to be a strong organization. That strength and that culture act as levers in addressing the multiple and seemingly insurmountable challenges that come along."[10]

What are some of the downsides to model 3 approaches? One has been replication. A few social businesses, including Muhammad Yunus's Grameen, have managed both to replicate and to inspire much larger organizations (among them, Citibank) to follow their lead, but most have so far proved harder to replicate than mainstream businesses. While they are certainly scalable, as their track records clearly show, and are scaling, replicating Sekem and La Fageda in other contexts is tough. In fact, it has yet to be done.

A number of reasons make replication challenging. For one, the problems Sekem and La Fageda are addressing are complicated. Furthermore, these businesses have to be profitable, or they can't survive. It would be much easier for Abouleish and Colón to be regular entrepreneurs; then, the only driver would be the financial bottom line. No wonder the conventional business world views people like them as unreasonable. But perhaps replication is not the real issue here. How about inspiration? In Egypt and in Spain, Abouleish and Colón have achieved almost Yunus-like status. They have demonstrated that there is another alternative (indeed, Abouleish was the 2005 recipient of the Right Livelihood Award, sometimes described as the "alternative Nobel Prize").

For these organizations to achieve wider replication, market conditions must change, funding sources must evolve, and the financial markets (from investors and lenders through risk takers and insurers) must adapt to the needs of these new actors. We examine the question of how such entrepreneurs raise funding and other resources for their ventures in the next chapter. Before we do, however, let's take a quick look at one business with a social mission that has grown and replicated at a tremendous rate and is now a publicly traded company.

Achieving Scale as a Social Business: Whole Foods

With some thirty-nine thousand employees, Whole Foods Market is on an altogether different scale than enterprises like Sekem. Founded in 1980 as a single small store in Austin, Texas, it is now the world's leading retailer of natural and organic foods, with nearly two hundred stores in North America and the United Kingdom. Its success is monitored by tracking customer satisfaction, team excellence and happiness, return on capital investment, improvement in the state of the environment, and local and larger community support. Operating at the interface between model 3 organizations and the business mainstream, Whole Foods indicates the potential for some social business models to scale and replicate.

Given that Whole Foods' founder John Mackey says that many of his former colleagues thought that he had gone to the "dark side" when he began to scale his business, it is worth asking why Whole Foods is a social business. One part of the answer is that it has done a great deal to drive whole food and organic food concepts into the commercial mainstream. Mackey would probably be the first to accept that there is big chasm between model 3 ventures and fully fledged, publicly listed enterprises with a social purpose, but his story suggests that the ripples of unreasonableness are spreading. As we shall see, it also shows that even those who claim to fight for social or environmental issues may still have their dark sides.

Mackey erupted into the spotlight in 2007 when reports emerged that he had been using anonymous postings on an investors' online message board to attack Wild Oats Markets, a firm that Whole Foods hoped to acquire. The Federal Trade Commission had blocked the proposed $565 million takeover on competitive grounds, and Mackey then faced a U.S. Securities and Exchange Commission inquiry into the postings. Mackey's initial belligerent response soon morphed into a public apology—coupled with a plea for stakeholders' forgiveness. (This was not new behavior: Mackey admitted that he had been posting anonymously over nine years.) People

who knew Mackey might have been surprised that he had so egre-
giously infringed on Whole Foods' core value of integrity—something he had touted often in public—but no doubt they would also
have concluded that his behavior reflected the forthright personal-
ity that had done so much to push the company forward.

Before the scandal, Mackey had made much of the fact that he
had come full circle from the antibusiness zealotry that fuels social
activists, and he stressed that he considered Whole Foods the better
for it. Whichever way you look at him, Mackey has always been a
very different kettle of fish from the social entrepreneurs we've profiled to this point, some of whom might think *him* unreasonable.

Like other social entrepreneurs, however, Mackey has been the
mainspring of the business, which made the scandal even more damaging.[11] Earlier in his career, he had noted that before founding
Whole Foods, he attended two different universities but "ended up
with no degree." He explained:

> I never took a single business class. I actually think that has
> worked to my advantage in business. I spent my late teens and
> early twenties trying to discover the meaning and purpose of
> my own life. My search for meaning and purpose led me into
> the counter-culture movement of the late 1960s and 1970s. I
> studied eastern philosophy and religion at the time, and still
> practice both yoga and meditation. I studied ecology. I became a
> vegetarian (I am currently a vegan), I lived in a commune, and I
> grew my hair and beard long. I'm one of those crunchy-granola
> types. Politically, I drifted to the Left and embraced the ideology
> that business and corporations were essentially evil because they
> selfishly sought profits. I believed that government was "good"
> (if the "right" people had control of it) because it altruistically
> worked for the public interest.[12]

Mackey's first steps included launching his own business in
1978, a natural foods market called Safer Way, a small store that
he opened with his girlfriend, with an initial $45,000 in capital.

"We were very idealistic, and we started the business because we thought it would be fun," he recalls. Idealistic he may be, but Mackey is no friend of left-wing politics these days. "At the time I started my business," he says, "the Left had taught me that business and capitalism were based on exploitation: exploitation of consumers, workers, society and the environment. I believed that 'profit' was a necessary evil at best, and certainly not a desirable goal for society as a whole."

Mackey's experience with Safer Way completely changed his life:

Everything I believed about business was proven to be wrong. The most important thing I learned about business in my first year was that business wasn't based on exploitation or coercion at all. Instead, I realized that business is based on voluntary co-operation. No one is forced to trade with a business; customers have competitive alternatives in the market place; employees have competitive alternatives for their labor; investors have different alternatives and places to invest their capital. Investors, labor, management, suppliers—they all need to cooperate to create value for their customers. If they do, then any realized profit can be divided amongst the creators of the value through competitive market dynamics. In other words, business is not a zero sum game with a winner and loser. It is a win, win, win, win game.

That, at least was the theory. Mackey says:

However, I discovered despite my idealism that our customers thought our prices were too high, our employees thought they were underpaid, the vendors would not give us large discounts, the community was forever clamoring for donations, and the government was slapping us with endless fees, licenses, fines and taxes. Were we profitable? Not at first. Safer Way managed to lose half of its capital in the first year—$23,000. Despite the loss, we were still accused of exploiting our customers with high prices and our employees with lower wages. The investors weren't making a profit and we had no money to donate. Plus, with our losses, we paid no taxes. I had somehow joined the "dark side." According to the perspective of the Left, I had become a greedy and selfish businessman.

At this point, Mackey chose to abandon the leftist philosophy of his youth because it no longer adequately explained how he thought the world really worked. So does he still agree, as he did when he was young, with Milton Friedman's view that "there is one and only one social responsibility of business—to use its resources and engage in activities designed to increase its profits so long as it stays within the rules of the game, which is to say, engages in open and free competition without deception or fraud"?[13] No, Mackey insists:

That's the orthodox view among free market economists: that the only social responsibility a law-abiding business has is to maximize profits for the shareholders. I strongly disagree. I'm a businessman and a free market libertarian, but I believe that the enlightened corporation should try to create value for *all* of its constituencies. From an investor's perspective, the purpose of the business is to maximize profits. But that's not the purpose for other stakeholders—for customers, employees, suppliers, and the community. Each of those groups will define the purpose of the business in terms of its own needs and desires, and each perspective is valid and legitimate.[14]

Whether or not you subscribe to his politics, Mackey has certainly built a substantial model 3 business and has moved it into the business mainstream. "In 2005, [Whole Foods Market] did $4.7 billion in sales and realized $136 million in net profits," he noted a couple of years ago. "With our current growth rates by 2010 we should do over $12 billion in sales. On a percentage basis, Whole Foods Market is the most profitable public food retailing business in the United States, with the highest net profit percentage, sales growth, and sales per square foot." But, he stresses, that isn't the end of the story. "I believe that business has a much greater purpose," he explains. "Business, working through free markets, is possibly the greatest force for good on the planet today. When executed well, business increases prosperity, ends poverty, improves the quality of life, and promotes the health and longevity of the world population at an unprecedented rate."[15]

Whether his postings about Wild Oats over those nine years were simply a case of a high-octane entrepreneur blowing off steam or a conscious effort to drive down the price of a takeover target, Mackey's story remains something of an exception among model 3 ventures, but it hints at the approach's potential. Given that the very nature of capitalism makes many such experiments fail and that all experience wobbles along the way, it remains to be seen how Whole Foods and other social businesses fare in the long run. But as publicly traded companies focus more on social and environmental objectives alongside their financial requirements, social businesses could gain greater prominence in serving the expanding markets of social and environmental needs.

Each of the three models described can be used to address any of the great social and environmental divides we explore in chapter 3—and the market opportunities they reveal. Remember, too, that individual entrepreneurs may move between models—and, over time, a given enterprise may morph from one business model to another, as several of our examples have done. In every model and for every market need these models seek to address, however, entrepreneurs must raise funding and gather other resources, a subject to which we now turn.

TWO

Tapping Financial Resources

WHATEVER MODEL THEY USE, and whether they set up their ventures as for-profits or nonprofits, even the most successful entrepreneurs can soon find themselves on a nonstop treadmill where they spend every waking moment chasing money. Often, this can be at the expense of using their talents to strengthen the impact of their ventures. As Richard Jefferson, founder of the open source biotechnology organization Cambia, remarked, "I can no longer be the playwright, the director and the principal actor." [1] But so it goes. As organizations scale, the role of the entrepreneur changes—as does the nature, scale, and availability of the needed funding.

The very definition of an entrepreneur is someone who "shifts economic resources out of an area of lower production into an area of higher yield and production," according to Jean-Baptiste Say, who is credited with coining the term *entrepreneurship*.[2] Social entrepreneurs who aim to transform communities almost inevitably operate under significant financial constraints, yet this might actually work in their favor, by forcing them to leverage the resources of the people they are trying to serve and, in the process, empowering those people to take charge of their own transformational process, on their own terms. This is not an argument for starving such entrepreneurs of resources but for understanding the particular models of transformation that the best of them use.

Take Joe Madiath from Gram Vikas, who works in Orissa, one of the poorest states in India and home to those most marginalized on the Indian social ladder: the tribal peoples. He has directly transformed the lives of two hundred thousand adults and children with just $6 million of capital each year. But he is able to leverage an additional $32 million from the contributions that each family in the participating tribal village provides to a "corpus" or community fund, which holds endowments or equity investments for future development projects that the community wants to embark on. Gram Vikas provides the technical expertise in water and sanitation and supports the community development process for about five years. Gram Vikas staff live in the villages during the process. In this example, tapping financial resources is about leverage from the bottom up, and Madiath leverages over five times the capital that he mobilizes from his basic donor community.

Despite such success stories, wherever you go in the world, most social entrepreneurs (and many environmental entrepreneurs) are acutely aware of the problem of the "missing middle"—the gap between the traditional funding of nonprofit ventures through grants, usually limited in size and excluding operational costs, and the more substantial financial investments necessary for rapid expansion. Experience shows that those organizations that manage to grow rapidly tend to focus on a single source of funding—for example, U.S. nonprofits tend to turn to the government for grants.[3] Other entrepreneurs take on debt, but doing so can be a mixed blessing in terms of supporting scale-up and replication. As Martin Fisher from KickStart puts it, "Why should I take on debt? I then have to go look for grants to pay it off."[4] Others have also observed a debt paradox—where social entrepreneurs take on debt to fund expansion, with the unintended effect of slowing their growth as they focus on servicing interest and paying down the debt.

Whichever model entrepreneurs choose, most soon look for advice from specialists on how to handle the financial side of their ventures. In some parts of the world, they are almost spoiled by the sheer number of choices.[5] What follows in this chapter, therefore, is not a step-by-step guide to money management or financial planning. Instead, we explore some of the more interesting trends in resource mobilization for social and environmental ventures. In each case, we spotlight one or more entrepreneurs and their relevant experience and lessons learned.

In general, all enterprises—including the most profit-hungry mainstream ventures—start out as nonprofits, whether or not they are legally constituted as such. (It took Amazon over five years to turn a profit, for example.) But an enterprise's ability to access traditional capital market mechanisms that allow it to grow depends on whether it is set up as a for-profit or a nonprofit. For the former, accessing financing can be relatively straightforward, although never easy. For nonprofits, there are fewer options, with social entrepreneurs, both the great and the mediocre, competing for a limited pool of funds. Consequently, these entrepreneurs have to be creative and arm themselves with persuasive business plans accompanied by a list of deliverables and timelines as they set out to find resources for their ventures.

Nonprofits tend to keep to the options outlined first in this chapter, from tapping foundations to conjuring up in-kind resources. Some are adapting growth models from the for-profit sector, including making sales and franchising, but their legal structure bars them from seeking funds from the capital markets. For-profits push toward more mainstream routes to finance, often attracting various forms of venture capital, and going public.

A major survey by Columbia Business School, the Investors' Circle, and Social Venture Network clarified the prevailing patterns among some two thousand U.S. for-profit social and environmental entrepreneurs. Over two hundred CEOs replied, and the average size of the firms proved to be very small, with more than 75 percent having fewer than twenty-five full-time employees.[6] Most of the CEOs thought that their companies could scale without sacrificing values or priorities, the first of which was "improving the environment," followed by "improving health and developing communities." Most had been financed to date by money from founders, family and friends, and angel investors. While some firms had used bank debt and institutional equity financing, including venture capital, as for-profit ventures they were much less likely to use foundation grants and similar sources of funding available to nonprofit enterprises. Most of these social venture CEOs reported that they planned to continue holding their companies privately, although attitudes toward acquisition and going public varied considerably by sector.

The fundamental challenge that all such entrepreneurs face is persuading the rest of the world—particularly potential funders—that their basic concept is both important and viable. When we asked some of the top social entrepreneurs what advice they would give young people starting out in the field, Barry Coleman of Riders for Health suggested that they should "put a decorated, framed copy on [their] office wall citing the social entrepreneurs' call to action: 'It can't be done!' "[7] The power of the unreasonable people profiled in these pages flows from their recognition that it can—indeed, must—be done. But, while we like the sentiment expressed in the title of a book by Coffee Republic founders Sahar and Bobby Hashemi—*Anyone Can Do It*—it really can't be done by just anyone.[8] The people we spotlight truly are a rare breed.

So how do the successful ones do it? To find out, SustainAbility carried out a quantitative survey for the Skoll Foundation of over one hundred leading entrepreneurs around the world.[9] We were closely involved in the project, Elkington as head of the project, Hartigan as a member of the project advisory panel. The size of the sample does not permit in-depth analysis of the funding approaches of different types of enterprises, but it does provide a useful sense of the overall trends. Given the scale of respondents' ambitions, it is hardly surprising that almost all of them felt re-source constrained, with many expressing a need to diversify their sources of funding. It was clear that raising money is the single-greatest challenge entrepreneurs face, with "access to capital" the most mentioned issue in the survey (by 72 percent of respondents). And there are no easy answers. "All sources of money come with their own challenges," as one entrepreneur put it. Figure 2-1 shows the sources of money and other resources these entrepreneurs re-ported relying on; figure 2-2 shows the sources they think they will be tapping five years in the future.

Nearly every entrepreneur also noted the importance of time frames. In particular, the work they are engaged in tends to be longer term (five to ten years to results was typical) and requires consistent long-range partnerships and funding. Access to flexible funding was also a consistent theme: most entrepreneurs are able to obtain specific project financing, but they have a harder time ac-cessing funds that will support more general infrastructure needs.

FIGURE 2-1

Preferred sources of funding

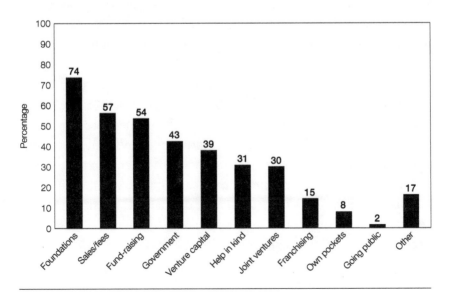

FIGURE 2-2

Sources of funding in five years

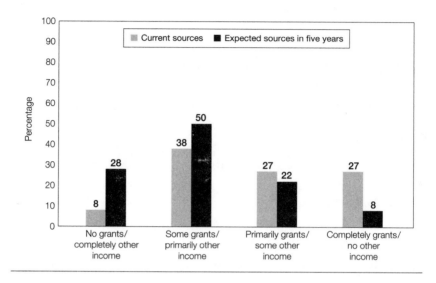

The survey's overriding conclusion was that the unique ap-proaches of social entrepreneurs are hard to fit into existing investor models and criteria, although the same point probably could be made about all forms of entrepreneurship. Foundations and gov-ernments tend to be siloed and conservative; as a result, they strug-gle to take on grantees that don't fit their narrow sense of solution options. Worse, these groups generally do not lend to for-profit organizations, which leaves out a significant number of social and environmental entrepreneurs. Traditional debt instruments are some-times used, but as already noted, they can present major challenges because entrepreneurs have to service the debt. Current equity in-vestments are shorter term than what is needed—and are often too expensive for entrepreneurs with a social mission.

We found entrepreneurs following one or more of the following ten routes to money. The descriptions in this chapter are sequenced in the order a typical entrepreneur might try them out, but the actual ranking by frequency of reported use was rather different, with foundations at the top, followed by sales/fees, public fund-raising, and governments.[10] The question we asked entrepreneurs was this: "Thinking about financing your initiatives, which sources of funding do you think will be the best avenues for you to pursue?"

For ventures structured as nonprofits (leveraged and hybrid nonprofits), foundations turn out to be the top funding source today, at least for those in the sample. That said, one of the most striking findings was the remarkable collapse in the number of entrepreneurs expecting to rely completely on grants in five years—from 27 percent today to 8 percent five years out. On the other side of the equation, there was an equivalent jump in those expecting to fund their own operations with no reliance on grants—up from 8 percent to 28 percent. In the middle ground, we saw a somewhat less dramatic fall in the proportion of respondents saying that they expect to still rely on grants with some income (from 27 percent to 22 percent) and a more striking growth in the proportion expecting a significant rebalancing in favor of earned income (from 38 percent to 50 percent).

Let's run through the sequence of funding sources to get a sense of what is keeping today's social and environmental entrepreneurs airborne, apart from sheer will and personal momentum.

Fishing in Back Pockets

Many mainstream entrepreneurs start out tapping the resources of their families and friends—although only 8 percent of our respondents checked this box. Given that few social entrepreneurs have the money to finance a venture using their savings or credit cards, it was no great surprise to find that this was the second-least-preferred option. Those who had considered tapping friends and family sources generally decided to avoid it because it comes with such intense personal pressure.

An example of such strains on family relationships comes from Brazil and has a happy ending. When Vera Cordeiro decided to leave her position as a pediatrician at the Lagoa Hospital in Rio de Janeiro to set up Renascer, she found herself looking at every family member and friend as a potential contributor. Cordeiro decided to leave after despairing about what seemed like the hospital's revolving door, through which the same children were readmitted time and again. She realized that, as a doctor, she had no cure for the poverty that was making them sick. Rather, a host of nonmedical interventions was needed to improve their health—including nutrition, housing, and securing jobs for caretakers (in most cases, mothers who headed the household).

Cordeiro, clearly an unreasonable woman, invested all her savings to launch Renascer. When that was not enough, she started invading her teenage daughters' closets and selling their clothes. The girls even ended up installing padlocks to ward off further raids. But when her husband Paolo's gold Rolex watch disappeared, he walked out. Cordeiro steeled herself and struggled on, slowly rallying a growing army of individuals from middle-class Brazil and their companies to deploy skills and products in the service of poor children and families. Eventually, Renascer took off (and, in time, Paolo returned and now works with Cordeiro). Most significantly, perhaps, the Renascer model has been replicated at seventeen Brazilian sites, each of which supports a hospital that refers chronically sick children for help.

The handful of people who reported taking this route to money in our survey did see at least one key advantage: those using their own money tended to practice intense financial discipline. That said, a striking number of internationally known social entrepreneurs seem to come from relatively well-off backgrounds. Craig Cohon, for example, has invested a good deal of his own money in Globalegacy, his network of business, nongovernmental organizations (NGOs), and development practitioners who are developing new ways to use market-based enterprises to address poverty and sustainability issues. Asked where the initial funding came from, he replied, "I put in $200,000 from my back pocket, as well attracting $200,000 of in-kind support from the Monitor Group and another $100,000 from [the UK law firm] Freshfields."[11] Cohon, who had previously worked for Coca-Cola and helped set up the beverage company's Russian business, says that he was "determined to start this as a business and ensure that funders had equity." That approach remains very rare in the social space, though it is much more common in the cleantech sector, where for-profit models rule.

Raising Funds from the Public

Public fund-raising just squeaked into third place, at 54 percent, with entrepreneurs underscoring the independence derived from money raised in this fashion. Fund-raising events are more common in some countries than others, with U.S. groups particularly likely to go this route. Celebrities are often used to draw in potential givers or investors, and few celebrities have been more successful than Bob Geldof in garnering media coverage and getting through to ordinary people. Although he may not like it, Geldof is now much better known for his work on campaigns like Band Aid, Live Aid, Live 8, and Make Poverty History than he is for his time as front man for the Boomtown Rats, which is funny because the Rats' first single was "Lookin' After Number One."

Eventually, the Band Aid brand proved highly versatile. In 2005, for example, Geldof announced the Live 8 project to raise awareness of issues that burden Africa—among them, government debt, trade barriers, and HIV/AIDS. He organized concerts in London, Paris, Berlin, Philadelphia, and Barrie, Ontario. In the run-up to the G8 Gleneagles summit, he fronted British Prime Minister Tony Blair's Commission for Africa, emphasizing public-private partnerships, free trade, and foreign direct investment. Although Gleneagles was praised as "the greatest summit for Africa ever" by the UN secretary-general, many aid agencies were disappointed. Indeed, figures released in 2007 showed that aid given to the poorest countries by the richest fell by $5.5 billion from the previous year.[12] But Geldof kept up the pressure, criticizing the world's richest countries for falling short on their pledges.[13]

Another celebrity from the music industry, Peter Gabriel, was the driving force behind Witness, the human rights organization led by Gillian Caldwell. Gabriel was able to galvanize his counterparts, including Emmylou Harris and Chic, to raise money for and promote the venture. In Argentina, in a similar vein, Fútbol de las Estrellas (Soccer of the Stars) exploits the appeal of movie stars, singers, and soccer celebrities to attract media interest and win public support for a cultural center for disabled youngsters.

A different spin on the same principle works well for Linda Rottenberg, cofounder and CEO of Endeavor, an enterprising nonprofit that fosters business entrepreneurship in emerging markets. Rottenberg exploits the corporate and multilateral version of celebrity fund-raising. She has had little difficulty securing financial commitments from leading business entrepreneurs in Chile, Argentina, Brazil, Mexico, Uruguay, South Africa, Colombia, and Turkey—where Endeavor has set up country "spokes" that search for and select leading entrepreneurs.

U.S. funders have been less interested in supporting Endeavor's New York hub because the benefits of the organization's work accrue directly outside the United States. Still, Endeavor's work has proved highly appealing to corporate and multilateral backers that recognize the critical need for job-creating entrepreneurial ventures in emerging economies. So Rottenberg has built Endeavor's annual New York–based gala around honoring such people, including James Wolfensohn, former president of the World Bank; Sir Howard Stringer, chairman and CEO of Sony; and Jerry Wang and Terry Sernel of Yahoo! This raises about $1 million a year for Endeavor's global operations—and helps engage the corporate and multinational community.

In Mexico, meanwhile, social entrepreneur José Ignacio Avalos has been particularly ingenious in devising strategies to raise cash from the Mexican public for one of his nonprofit enterprises—Un Kilo de Ayuda (A Kilo of Help). He devised money cards that sell for less than a dollar. Each has a bar code that registers a donation for Un Kilo de Ayuda whenever the cardholder makes a purchase at a participating organization. The card's acceptance at more than twenty-five thousand points of sale across Mexico gives Un Kilo de Ayuda three times more coverage than other initiatives, including those run by Unicef.

Attracting Help in Kind

Although most entrepreneurs think in terms of raising financial support, in-kind resources often make up a major slice of the support nonprofit ventures end up attracting. Many donors—particularly businesses—find it easier to give in-kind support. Such help ranges from donations of surplus products (including books, carpets, and computers), sweat equity (in the form of volunteer labor), and pro bono services (such as the support many social entrepreneurs receive from such consultancies as Bain, The Boston Consulting Group, McKinsey, Monitor, and PricewaterhouseCoopers). In-kind donations came in sixth in our survey, at 31 percent, although volunteer effort and sweat equity were key resources for many. For example, Habitat for Humanity can build affordable houses for low-income families not just because the homes sell at cost and the mortgages are interest free but also because the construction involves extensive work from volunteers and the prospective homeowners.[14]

Some nonprofit social enterprises create revenues by taking in goods or equipment that others no longer have a use for, reconditioning them, and then making them available or selling them. In New York, Dress for Success and Career Gear collect suits and other business attire to help disadvantaged people dress for job interviews. The same approach is used by many other social entrepreneurs, notably those who ask companies for surplus IT equipment. The Committee for the Democratization of Information Technology uses donated equipment in some nine hundred computer schools in the slums of Brazil and other Latin American countries.

Increasingly, highly qualified professionals are interested in getting involved, offering their time and expertise. Some do so via their companies, which support and even encourage this work; others do so on their own initiative. Many social enterprises are becoming more and more discriminating in picking even expert volunteers, recognizing the critical importance of the quality of the support and services provided. In the Czech Republic, for example, a social enterprise called Bílý Kruh Bezpeči offers counseling and aftercare to victims of violent crime. To ensure its services are of high quality, the organization specifically aims to pull in well-trained psychologists and lawyers.

McKinsey's support for Ashoka—whose founder, Bill Drayton, spent seven years at the firm—is higher profile. In fact, it was McKinsey's values that drew Drayton to the firm in the first place. "I came to McKinsey because I felt it was an institution that had as its goal causing real and important change to take place," he has recalled. "Causing significant change is different than just being brilliant."[15] This pairing of values and a desire for positive change resulted in the Ashoka-McKinsey Center for Social Entrepreneurship, established in Brazil in 1996, following a pro bono study for Ashoka. In this venture Ashoka identifies potential industry-defining leaders in the social sector with powerful strategies and strong organizations. McKinsey then helps these leaders build strategic and management skills, with the partnership now extending to fourteen countries.

Appealing to Angels and Foundations

Foundations, as already mentioned, came in first place (74 percent) for entrepreneurs working in the nonprofit field. Despite some frustrations, those relying on foundations—in whole or in part—see them as a dependable funding source. One advantage in countries like the United States was articulated by Jim Fruchterman, president of Benetech in the SustainAbility survey: "There are the advantages of size in the case of foundations and very rich people. An amount of effort is likely to land $250,000."[16]

Some respondents mentioned that they were trying to change their focus from foundations to high-net-worth individuals—partly because they felt this was an untapped source, partly because they expected that such funding might come with fewer conditions. Successfully cultivating such relationships may take a good deal of effort, but they provide the bedrock on which organizations can build other fund-raising. "Over sixteen years, we have built up a donor base of foundation and individual funders who are very loyal to our organization and give year after year," said the Nepalese Youth Opportunity Foundation in the SustainAbility survey.

The tide has been moving in angel investors' favor. "Giving away money has never been so fashionable among the rich and famous," Matthew Bishop observed in the *Economist*.[17] Certainly, 2006, when his article appeared, will be remembered by some as the year when the second-richest man in the world (Warren Buffett) gave away his fortune to the richest (Bill Gates)—solely to expand the latter's philanthropic capacity. It is not an accident that both Buffett and Gates are American. The United States has long dominated the field of philanthropy. In 2004, for example, charitable giving rose by 5 percent to a record $249 billion, representing over 2 percent of GDP, according to the Giving USA Foundation.[18] Both in absolute terms and as a proportion of GDP, that money was more than any other industrialized country gave to charity.

History and culture are among the reasons why the country leads the world in philanthropic giving. People like Carnegie, Rockefeller, and Ford established a culture of "giving back," a guilt-laden expression, suggesting the need to atone for the "crime" of having amassed vast wealth. Some of that guilt may well have been warranted, given that much of the wealth came at the expense of individuals, society, and the environment. Whatever the motivation, the United States has long benefited from setting well-defined rules and regulations to facilitate and encourage its population to contribute to charity. Those incentives include substantial tax exemptions, both for those who carry out the charitable work under 501(c)(3) status and for the philanthropists who contribute to such organizations.

Over time, other leading countries have adopted similar incentives. As a result, those looking for business angels know that they now come in many forms—including independently wealthy people, those who run independent foundations, and the superphilanthropists. From Bill and Melinda Gates to the founders of companies like eBay and Google, a new wave of wealthy people are bankrolling social and environmental entrepreneurs. There are thought to be around 600 billionaires worldwide, with a small but growing handful plunging into the field of venture philanthropy.[19]

Billionaire George Soros, who emerged early in the field, describes the network of organizations he finances as "a cross between a foundation and a movement."[20] As the *Financial Times* noted, that movement "has subsidized ministers' salaries in Georgia after the Rose Revolution, saved scientists in the former Soviet Union from starvation and seeks to promote government transparency, human rights and a free press."[21] The initiatives undertaken by such people have profound longer-term implications not only for the world's poor and those fighting such problems as disease, corruption, and climate change but also for mainstream business and financial markets. Often, people like Soros have either made their money elsewhere or inherited it and, as a result, are less concerned about immediate financial returns than mainstream investors. But they are not naive—some also have an eye on the longer-term prospects of profitability once new markets are established.

Around the same time that Soros was getting into his stride, billionaire Swiss entrepreneur and industrialist Stephan Schmidheiny was founding Avina.[22] Having worked for decades with big companies, Schmidheiny became interested in entrepreneurial solutions to the world's great problems. He explained:

For me, a good entrepreneur is someone who consistently develops [his or her] business with a clear vision and an equally clear mission, works very hard, and has a special ability to efficiently administer the capital, the resources and the technology available.

An entrepreneur is someone capable of persuading others to adopt [his or her] own vision, of motivating them to achieve [his or her] goals. However, the entrepreneur I now imagined would not have to build huge companies but rather bring about positive change that would afford as many people as possible the opportunity to lead decent, dignified and productive lives and to change the regional economy situation.[23]

In a moment of serendipity, Schmidheiny stumbled across Bill Drayton and Ashoka when reading a magazine during a transatlantic flight. He soon built a partnership with Ashoka, using his capital to help fund its programs, particularly those in Latin America. Schmidheiny recalled: "The success of Ashoka's entrepreneurs proved to me that heads of government and captains of industry—those who should actually be responsible for improving their societies—seldom bring about significant changes. The secret lies in searching for individuals with leadership abilities, not only among the so-called elites, but in all sectors of society."[24]

Some social entrepreneurs have been successful in winning one or more of the growing number of corporate foundation awards. Barefoot College, for example, won the $1 million Alcan Prize for Sustainability in 2006. Developed in partnership with the International Business Leaders Forum, the prize is awarded to "any not-for-profit, civil society or nongovernmental organization based anywhere in the world that is demonstrating a comprehensive approach to addressing, achieving and further advancing economic, environmental and/or social sustainability."[25]

Tapping the Government

Many social entrepreneurs provide goods and services to people that conventional government agencies struggle to reach, so it is no surprise that a fair number seek public sector finance and support. In fact, turning to the government for funding was favored by a significant proportion of entrepreneurs, coming in fourth place at 43 percent. Even for-profit entrepreneurs saw public sector agencies as a key funding source. "They represent the shortest paths to the level of funding we require," said a representative from one solar photovoltaics company.

While some using government funding noted upsides—such as collaborating with leading scientists at government laboratories, public relations benefits, and access to government procurement sources—others were frustrated by the significant constraints associated with government funding and its prescriptive nature. Because government agencies remain accountable to the general public, they are often much less able to offer the kind of flexible funding guidelines that most social or environmental ventures need.

Many social enterprises do not invest the same effort in developing close relationships with governments as they do with businesses, but there are a growing number of them that do. One enterprise that illustrates the possibilities is the Childline India Foundation (CIF), which was started to provide a free telephone helpline to the deprived street children of Bombay. CIF persuaded the government that it could provide services that the government should have been supplying—and ended up getting the relevant ministry's backing for a bold expansion plan to cover over forty Indian cities.

Another entrepreneur who has tapped government funding is Tim Smit, the driving force behind the United Kingdom's extraordinary Eden Project, which welcomed its eight-millionth visitor in 2006.[26] A giant ecological theme park, housed in a series of domes that mushroom out of the floor of an old clay quarry in Cornwall, Eden employs five hundred people and is estimated to have attracted over $1.2 billion of spending to the county, the poorest in the country. While the $230 million project has already taken $170 million in public funding to get off the ground, it could considerably open out its funding by accepting corporate sponsorship of Eden's major features. Smit has been wary of taking this route, however. The big phone companies have been itching to get involved, he says, "but we would lose something if we accepted their dough."[27]

Making Sales and Charging Fees

The Eden Project is already generating significant income through sales, entry fees, and membership subscriptions, even if the funds raised are insufficient to cover total costs. Earning income marks a clear watershed as entrepreneurs and their organizations move toward the for-profit model. Indeed, sales and fees are critical steps toward financial sustainability because they help nonprofit and for-profit ventures alike move from "fossil" sources of money (in the sense that wealth is laid down in dense, energy-rich seams in foundations) to renewable sources.

Over half (57 percent) of respondents preferred to draw some of their revenues from sales and fees, which came in second in our survey. One respondent, Jim Fruchterman of Benetech, noted, "Earned income is a mark of the value of your product—and provides feedback from your customers." Earning income is easier in markets that are working (to some degree, at least) than where there are clear market failures. Some of those surveyed saw their sector as much less likely to generate sales and fees. "Education is an area where there is a lower expectation of profitability," as the Fascinating Learning Factory put it.

A few respondents mentioned a tension at the heart of social entrepreneurship: on the one hand, there is a desire to give away information for free; on the other, there is a need to earn revenue to be sustainable. "We've not yet worked out a way to earn income from selling our knowledge," said EarthLink in the SustainAbility survey. "In the recent book *The Spider and the Starfish*, the role of an intermediary, or catalyst, was described. Such people have a difficult time earning income from ideas they give away to anyone who will listen. Our aim is to create a hybrid, where we draw people from around the world to our Web site because the causes we address are important to individuals, foundations, and people in industry, and we earn income by the types of services and tools we use to support the learning and interaction of these people."

When serving local populations in poor countries, social entrepreneurs must tailor their offerings to the needs and pockets of the disadvantaged. So, for example, Bangladesh's Waste Concern is fighting the mountains of garbage in Dhaka by collecting and recycling organic waste. Operating in low-income neighborhoods and slums, the organization has demonstrated that the approach works and creates jobs. In the process, it has discovered that people in slum areas are willing to pay for the waste collection service.[28] Better still, Waste Concern sells the compost resulting from the recycling processes to fertilizer companies. Continuing this virtuous cycle, these companies then make an organic, environment-friendly fertilizer and sell that to farmers at a very low cost.

Some social entrepreneurs use a differential pricing model for their products and services, with the better-off charged more and the less well-off charged significantly less or, in some cases, nothing. Consider David Green of Project Impact, who has been successful in getting low-cost health products, including cataract implant lenses and surgical sutures, to millions of poor people in developing countries. He is also now focusing on creating local capacity to manufacture and sell affordable hearing aids. To make this work, he has introduced a pricing system based on the customer's ability to pay. The poorest customers receive products for free, a service made possible by charging better-off customers more than the cost of the product—but still significantly less than they would pay for competing products.

Membership fees are another route to money. This approach is adopted by India's Self-Employed Women's Association (SEWA), a trade union for women working as vendors, as artisans, as salt workers, or otherwise on their own account. SEWA fights for these women's rights and offers services ranging from health care to microcredit and insurance. It asks for a small membership fee and has over half a million paying members.

A developed-world counterpart, meanwhile, is the Freelancers Union started by Working Today, founded by Sara Horowitz. The Freelancers Union represents the needs and concerns of America's growing independent workforce through advocacy, information, and services. These independent, self-employed workers—free-lancers, consultants, independent contractors, temps, part-timers, and contingent employees—currently make up about 30 percent of the U.S. workforce. To make sure that independent workers have access to health insurance and other benefits, Working Today has built relationships with professional associations, membership- and community-based organizations, unions, and companies. That way, the organization is able to reach large numbers of independent workers, giving them access to services and essential products previously available only to the traditional workforce of full-time, long-term employees.

Franchising

Franchising seemed to be somewhat outside the mainstream for the entrepreneurs in our survey, coming in eighth place (15 percent), but it is at least on the map. An example of a social enterprise that may franchise is Amsterdam-based Aflatoun, also known as Child Savings International, which has been considering franchising its Aflatoun brand to banks and other financial institutions. The organization's founder and chair, Indian serial social entrepreneur Jeroo Billimoria, is pursuing a dual-level franchise model where one level addresses nonprofits and the other for-profits. On the for-profit side, where the aim is to partner with banks, she is setting up Aflatoun Inc., which will own the brand and open up the option of raising money through capital markets.

Many activist organizations and other nonprofits have evolved versions of franchising, including the World Wildlife Fund (or World Wide Fund for Nature, as it is known outside North America), human rights campaigners Amnesty International, anticorruption proponents Transparency International, and Habitat for Humanity. And there is a growing interest in experimentation. Jean Horstman, CEO of InnerCity Entrepreneurs, told us, "We are in the process of testing out licensing as the way to scale our impact quickly while growing our organization at a reasonable pace. We are exploring creating branches in the state of Massachusetts to learn to scale at the state level, while licensing our curriculum and support services nationally."[29]

Franchising is significantly more likely to work on the for-profit side, however, and has been adopted on a larger scale by for-profit social entrepreneurs. Most of those entrepreneurs founded their companies in part to drive a social mission—and many have managed to remain true to that mission, despite major challenges along the way. So what gets such people into the world of business and, in many cases, franchising? The stories differ, but they share common threads. Orb Energy, for example, is franchising to scale its operations in India, preferring this route rather than raising additional capital. The franchise branches enable the organization to get closer to customers, while establishing a common look and feel and affording greater economies of scale. A key challenge in this approach, as CEO Damian Miller told us, is ensuring that franchisees do not sacrifice quality for revenues.

Another example is the Body Shop. The company's DNA was unusual from the outset and is summarized in its mission statement: "To dedicate our business to the pursuit of social and environmental change." The challenges that the Body Shop's late founder, Anita Roddick, and her husband and business partner, Gordon, faced were legion, as the company's sheer size today indicates. The Body Shop became "a multi-local business with [2,100 in 2007] stores serving over 77 million customers in 51 different markets in 25 different languages and across 12 time zones."[30] Roddick herself commented, "I haven't a clue how we got there!" A key part of the answer, however, is franchising.

Critics considered Anita Roddick unreasonable, even in late middle age. But entrepreneurs who, like her, take the for-profit route have one satisfaction denied their unreasonable counterparts working in the not-for-profit sector: they can cash in some of their shares—or sell out entirely. A growing number of social entrepreneurs have been traveling that route, which we examine toward the end of this chapter. The Roddicks publicly regretted their own IPO because it threatened to turn the Body Shop into a business like any other. They eventually sold out to L'Oréal, which was somewhat ironic given that Nestlé—one of the world's most boy-cotted firms—had a major stake in L'Oréal.

According to L'Oréal's chairman and chief executive, the business would remain independent, and its shares would no longer be listed. However, ratings agencies that track public perceptions of brands and company reputations were soon reporting that the Body Shop's favorability ratings had taken a significant knock. Roddick was rather more upbeat, however. "When you have the biggest cosmetics firm saying, 'We want you to teach us how to support small farms and women's cooperatives,' it is a very exciting moment." [31] She also noted that L'Oréal "could work with our Nicaraguan farmers who sell us 70 tons of sesame oil. How many tons could they use, a thousand? I mean, it's mind-blowing in terms of poverty eradication." [32] The proof, as her fellow Brits would put it, will be in the pudding.

Creating Partnerships and Joint Ventures

To scale up, most entrepreneurs must form partnerships or joint ventures—which makes it slightly surprising that less than a third (30 percent) of our respondents mentioned joint ventures as significant to their activities or plans. Those taking this route saw many potential nonfinancial benefits. Such partnerships, as noted on the Web site for Landmines Blow!, help both parties "leverage their assets, such as their expertise and client base, with other advantages including sharing knowledge, [cultivating] new relationships, developing a continuum of care, working successfully in different cultural settings, and [gaining] approval from the United States Federal Government and the United Nations." [33]

Those thinking about this option are concerned about the implications. "We have had a significant increase in companies wanting to sponsor us," said one entrepreneur, who asked to remain anonymous. "The challenge is to remain selective and not to sell out, to maintain the purity of our program." Many respondents wondered how they could learn to vet potential partners. Despite some social entrepreneurs' concerns about power imbalances, most of them often see mainstream businesses as the most interesting partners for a number of reasons. One is the sheer scale of the potential resources available in the corporate sector and the geographic reach and political influence of large companies. Another reason is entrepreneurs' growing appetite for understanding how to develop social and environmental initiatives on a more businesslike footing.

All over the world, companies are partnering with social entrepreneurs. Take Timberland, the maker of outdoor gear, which is traded on the New York Stock Exchange but is still owned by the founding family. Jeff Swartz, grandson of founder Nathan Swartz, took over as CEO in 1998 and recalls the moment when, some years earlier, he began to see the light. In 1991, he recalls, he was reading bible passages that his wife had given him. (As it happened, this was also the time that he had his first experience with City Year, in Boston.) "I thought: 'Oh boy, that's the text coming alive,'" he explains. "I felt the world moving under my feet, and I still do."[34] When he had his Road to Damascus conversion, Swartz not only part-owned Timberland but was also on track to take over as CEO. To some degree, the company was his to steer as he saw fit. Most companies and CEOs find themselves in different situations; in other cases, the partnerships involve a much lower degree of commitment by the mainstream company, even though the outcomes may be crucial for a given social enterprise.

The academic community's interest in partnerships and joint ventures is also growing. Jane Nelson, director of the corporate social responsibility initiative at Harvard University's Kennedy School of Government, has been one leading pioneer, exploring what succeeds—and what doesn't—when corporations join forces with the world of social entrepreneurship. In her work with Beth Jenkins, a senior consultant with Booz Allen Hamilton, Nelson has recommended that the business world expose more corporate leaders to social entrepreneurs through project visits, experiential learning, international forums, and integrating corporate responsibility and social entrepreneurship elements in mainstream business education.[35] Whether on the financial, management, or legal fronts, the need for brokering services seems likely to grow. We also need more companies that are willing to engage and invest in social and environmental entrepreneurs as part of their strategy, not just as part of their citizenship programs.

Pursuing Venture Capital

Venture capital ranked fairly high, in fifth place, with more than a third (39 percent) of respondents saying they plan to draw on some venture funding. This response is striking. It may be affected by the number of cleantech entrepreneurs in our sample or the fact that some social entrepreneurs fail to understand the nature of venture capital funding (specifically, venture capitalists typically expect high rates of return). Still, as entrepreneurs of every stripe drive toward mainstream markets, the stakes—and the prospects for longer-term profitability—will likely grow. As a result, venture capitalists, private equity funds, and other leading-edge financiers may become more interested.

Take one of the world's top venture capital firms: Kleiner Perkins Caufield & Byers (KPCB). As early investors in start-up companies like Amazon, Google, and Intuit, KPCB is widely seen as having a sensitive collective nose for the next big thing. It now spotlights such market drivers as looming energy-security issues, the growth of megacities, and the risk of abrupt climate change. As a result, it is emerging as a major player in the cleantech space.

Although the involvement of venture capitalists and investment bankers is necessary, there are clear risks for those who want to ensure that their business retains its social or environmental mission. To date, entrepreneurs who want to raise venture funding and to preserve their values have had relatively few choices, but they have had some.

Consider Triodos, Europe's leading ethical bank, based in the Netherlands. The bank was founded by four entrepreneurial individuals who came together in 1968 to think about how money could be managed in a socially conscious way. Triodos has tackled market opportunities neglected by other financial institutions and helped create new markets, including stimulating and supporting the development of alternative energy as a bankable sector. And Triodos has spread to the United Kingdom, Germany, Belgium, and Spain, focusing on companies and organizations that contribute to a better environment or generate social or cultural value added. Triodos manages venture capital funds and invests in social and environmental enterprises across Europe, targeting key sectors such as renewable energy, organic food, fair trade, clean technologies, culture, and integrated health. Since 2001, it has raised three venture capital funds totaling some $100 million.

One environmental enterprise Triodos has invested in, alongside the London-based venture capital firm zouk ventures, is the CarbonNeutral Company. Founded in 1990, the company—which helps citizens, business clients, and others offset their carbon emissions—has spanned the spectrum from celebrity-led public fundraising to venture capital and plans for an IPO. Ask the company's ex-CEO, Jonathan Shopley, what persuaded the company, once called Future Forests, to take the venture capital route, and he explains that the founders "were building not only a pioneering company but also a whole new low/no-carbon asset class for the economy."[36] He further notes that there was a need to scale fast.

Good venture capitalists, he points out, bring more than just money. "The upsides are clear," he says. "[Venture capitalists] can bring very powerful disciplines to bear. They provide invaluable counsel on the basis of huge experience. They understand risk and opportunity. And they can help you benchmark what you are doing against a wider field of high-potential businesses." What about the downsides? "The downside," he reflects, "is that you can end up having to give away what feels like a disproportionate share of the company in return for capital." Venture capital can also push entrepreneurs more rapidly than they might like toward an IPO or acquisition. "Venture capitalists need an exit strategy," Shopley concludes, "a way of realizing a return. This realization of value comes either via an IPO or—alternatively, particularly when a market is consolidating—via a trade sale to, or merger with, a bigger player." A sale or merger may lead to the next stage: an IPO.

Selling Out—or Going Public

People like Bill Drayton of Ashoka and Muhammad Yunus of the Grameen Group have called for social stock exchanges because the current setup is so poorly adapted for social entrepreneurs. And that showed in our survey results, where the option of going public appeared at the bottom of the heap (2 percent). The relatively slow progress of initiatives like the Global Exchange for Social Investment hasn't helped. As John Wood, founder and CEO of Room to Read, put it in the SustainAbility survey, "The capital markets for NGOs are blatantly inefficient. There is no mechanism that has the efficiency of the private sector [e.g., the New York Stock Exchange, Nasdaq, private placements, or venture capital] when it comes to raising large amounts of capital—especially unrestricted funding. The NGO world needs to have every large foundation seriously study—and, hopefully, emulate—this model." What is true for NGOs is also true for most model 1 and 2 social enterprises.

Once proof of concept is achieved, most entrepreneurs are eager to grow and replicate. Unfortunately, this is where too many come to a screeching halt or are forced to endure a painfully slow takeoff. Why? Despite a recent and unprecedented explosion of efforts to evolve the infrastructure needed to accelerate the flow of capital, considerably more capital is required to expand and strengthen replicable, innovative, and entrepreneurial organizations with social missions.

Part of the reason is because many of these entities, particularly if they're model 2 organizations, operate in some sort of limbo. They look too much like business for the more traditional philanthropically minded crowd, but when they turn to the business sector to

establish partnerships, they are often referred to the corporate social responsibility (CSR) department. Most philanthropists, like
most CSR programs, do not yet have the mind-sets (or, in most
cases, the capital) needed to help with scaling and replication, at
least where NGOs are concerned. John Wood said in the Sustain-
Ability survey, "Some organizations tell us that we have gotten
big, 'so you no longer need us.' " This reaction, he noted, "is very
different from the private sector, where success attracts capital.
Why should we be penalized for being successful, and why should
any investor want an organization they have supported in its early
years to remain small?"[37]

Certainly, a growing number of organizations are committed
to funding social enterprise. In fact, Ashoka, Echoing Green, New
Profit Inc., the Peninsula Community Foundation's Center for Venture Philanthropy, the Skoll Foundation, Social Venture Partners,
UnLtd, and Venture Philanthropy Partners are all investing more
than $1 million a year—in some cases, substantially more—in non-
profits. While these efforts are welcome, however, their collective
effort comes to less than $100 million a year, a relative drop in the
bucket.

To put very rough numbers on the three areas of social enterprise, cleantech, and philanthropy, we estimated in 2007 that less
than $200 million was going into social enterprise from dedicated
foundations, worldwide, compared with over $2 billion into clean-
tech in the United States and the European Union and well over
$200 billion into general philanthropy in the United States alone.

Overall, it is clear that any country that wants to build strong
clusters of social enterprise must make much larger amounts of
capital available, as well as other forms of financial and nonfinancial support. So if current capital markets don't work, an obvious—
if challenging—route is to set up your own. That was the idea
behind the Global Exchange for Social Investment. Launched with
much fanfare during the 2002 annual meeting of the World Economic Forum, this effort to create a global social capital market
had a fairly bumpy start.[38] Yet, as with pretty much all entrepre-

neurial endeavors, early setbacks can become future strengths if those at the helm embrace feedback and respond accordingly.

Another fledgling initiative in this area, the Social Stock Exchange (SSE), is based in Brazil and was launched by the Bolsa de Valores de São Paulo (aka Bovespa, the São Paulo Stock Exchange). Bovespa launched the SSE in 2003 to bring together nonprofit organizations with Bovespa investors who wished to support social efforts. As SSE creator Celso Grecco puts it, the donor is making a "social profit." Social organizations can submit their initiatives at any time. A team of experts reviews all the entries and recommends the most qualified to the SSE board. Once a proposal is approved, Bovespa and its 120 brokerage firms all over Brazil post the portfolio of initiatives to investors with the aim to sell these "social shares." All funds raised by the SSE go directly to the organization, without commissions or fees of any kind. The SSE promotes a new kind of ROI, a "return on inclusion." It seeks to create a new identity for NGOs, not as nonprofit organizations, but as "social profit organizations."

This initiative has generated considerable interest. In South Africa the experiment is being replicated through JSE Securities Exchange South Africa, which launched the South African Social Investment Exchange in June 2006. The exchange opened its initial offering with fifteen selected "social profit" projects. As in the SSE scheme, investors can purchase shares online and follow the progress of their investments via the Internet.

The challenge is much greater than such early experiments might suggest, however. As Muhammad Yunus has put it: "To enable a social stock-exchange to perform properly, we will need to create rating agencies, standardization of terminology, definitions, impact measurement tools, reporting formats, and new financial publications, such as *The Social Wall Street Journal.*"[39] So what makes mobilizing capital for proven social entrepreneurs so difficult? Part of the answer lies in a finding from a study by the law firm Linklaters with the Schwab Foundation: in no country has a coherent, specific legal model been developed for establishing social enterprises.[40]

At the root of this impasse lies the tendency across all countries and regions to separate out financial and social value. Currently, one segment of society is trying to maximize profits without much concern for the impact on the well-being of society as a whole, and another segment tries to deal with the fallout. Overall, the system is not working. It is time to change the rules of the game.

Part II

Creating the Markets
of the Future

THREE

Identifying Market Opportunities in Ten Great Divides

L IKE THE WRIGHT BROTHERS over a century ago, the duo of decidedly unreasonable bicycle makers who dreamed of lofting their machines into the realm of birds, today's social and environmental entrepreneurs see the possibility of helping people soar into the future where others see only insurmountable barriers. This optimism is somewhat uncharacteristic of the present, where looming, palpable threats continue to crop up—but that doesn't deter these entrepreneurs. In fact, the thought of impending doom may actually energize many of them.

Throughout history, people have acknowledged that dark clouds can have silver linings. "In the middle of every difficulty," Albert

Einstein is said to have observed, "lies opportunity." What distinguishes social entrepreneurs is not just their ability to see the potential opportunities created by challenges but also their leadership skills, which enable them to begin building the foundations of tomorrow's emerging markets and enterprises.

In the simplest terms, social and environmental entrepreneurs—whatever they intend—are helping build the business case for action in very different ways than their mainstream business and political counterparts. Show most mainstream companies the UN's Millennium Development Goals (MDGs), launched with great fanfare in 2000 and slated (with little chance of success) for completion by 2015, and they will tend to see endless problems in turning those goals into any sort of market reality.[1] True, a few companies are beginning to build their corporate reporting around particular MDGs, but they usually do so with a sense that because of the sheer scale of the challenges, their efforts will make relatively little impact. On the political front, 2015 sounds like someone else's problem, given the relatively short time horizons of democratic politics.

By contrast, show the MDGs to most social entrepreneurs, and many will note that their own ventures were addressing key issues years before the UN got around to laying out its own plans to address the ten great divides that our analysis suggests emerge from the MDGs and that we explore in this chapter. Many social entrepreneurs see the MDGs as much stronger on the what and why than on the who, how, where, and when. They ask disconcerting questions about what mainstream politicians, public agencies, businesses, and financial institutions are doing to achieve all these goals. Nevertheless, we find the divides identified in the MDGs a useful departure point for examining the issues and opportunities of the future.

Whatever their rhetoric, most leaders today tend to view these divides as virtually unbridgeable chasms. Analysts note that some of the divides are continuing to open, a phenomenon fueled in part by the very processes of globalization and wealth creation embedded in mainstream business models. We join leading social entrepreneurs in reframing the divides—which relate to demographics, finance, nutrition, access to finite natural resources, environment, health, gender, education, what we might call "digitech," and multiple forms of security—as pointers to tomorrow's market opportunity spaces.

To seize these opportunities, mainstream companies will have to stretch their thinking beyond the usual business case arguments for venturing into new and untested markets. Luckily, they can turn for guidance to social and environmental entrepreneurs—who are already operating in those markets, transforming products or processes in a number of ways. These entrepreneurs may be affecting supply chains, including shaping labor supply. They may be influencing or expanding the consumer base, either creating a demand for certain products among existing clients or tapping into a wholly new customer segment. Others may be acting as regulation forerunners, providing technology or services that foresee impending regulation and offering sustainable alternatives that can be adopted by businesses. Or they may be coming up with disruptive technologies that shift an entire industry by leapfrogging existing technology and making the *modus operandi* obsolete.

Let's run through all ten, briefly outlining the relevant challenges and then sketching some of the ways that social and environmental entrepreneurs are working to address them. In no case do the entrepreneurs—or even the entire sector—have the answers to the overall challenge, but at least their efforts to define solutions suggest a route toward the markets of the future.

Demographic Opportunities

Ultimately, demography is the fundamental driver of most—if not all—of the problems that these entrepreneurs are trying to tackle. The basic problem is one of numbers. Demographers tell us that the human population is headed toward 9 billion to 10 billion people sometime this century. Meanwhile, as if the growth in population numbers was not worrying enough, there is a different set of numbers we should pay attention to. Age distribution is skewing, with some nations aging and others experiencing a boom of young people. The pattern is predicted to intensify and complicate the world's political, economic, and social challenges. In parallel, a worldwide migration from rural areas to cities is occurring, and experts think that 2007 will prove to have been the year when humans became predominantly urban. That's good news for some, but for one in three people, that means living in a slum.[2]

For the entrepreneurially minded, all these problems can be—indeed, are—viewed as opportunities in disguise. Also on the positive side, recent decades have shown that one of the best ways of reining in population growth is encouraging economic development so that people no longer have to rely on large families to provide for their long-term social and economic well-being. This is the so-called demographic transition, and social entrepreneurs are addressing the many interrelated dimensions of this complex challenge. In doing so, they offer a variety of lessons for both the private and public sectors.

Taking population control first, consider Mechai Viravaidya (popularly known in Thailand as Dr. Condom). One of the lessons his success offers is that it helps to be able to spot serious challenges early—and to see their lighter side. Mechai established the Population and Community Development Association (PDA) in 1974 to tackle overpopulation, the root cause of poverty in his country. Now the largest Thai nongovernmental organization, PDA was the first such organization to use nonmedical personnel to distribute oral contraceptives and condoms in villages and cities. It also came up with creative and often humorous approaches to promote family planning, appealing to the Thai sense of fun and helping destigmatize reproductive matters.

Because of his condom-blowing contests and Miss Condom beauty pageants, Mechai also became known as the Condom King, and a condom became known as a "mechai." In the process, Thailand achieved one of the fastest fertility declines in modern times; the rate of annual population growth dropped from 3.3 percent in 1974 to just 0.8 percent by 2000, and the average number of children per family plummeted from seven to fewer than two. This is an extraordinary outcome by anyone's standards—and one that underscores the importance of these entrepreneurs' the-impossible-takes-a-little-longer mind-sets.

Mechai, however, is first and foremost a businessman. His fame as Dr. Condom did not come from a background in public health. Rather, on returning to his country after completing an MBA at the University of Melbourne, he was struck with the poverty of his fellow Thais. He quickly concluded that the situation would never change economically if Thailand's demographic profile did not change—that is, if women kept having between six and seven children. Thus, he set out to address the population explosion as a means to kick-start improvements in people's lives.

Mechai has always been a master at combining economic and social goals. PDA is a hybrid nonprofit venture that finances its activities through other social business ventures. Governments—and leading businesses—that are looking for solutions to demography-driven challenges can find a new set of levers in such enterprises, ensuring a bigger bang for their invested buck.

Second, and in a case that underscores this point, let's turn to entrepreneurial efforts designed to tackle problems created by populations skewing either to the young or old. One inspirational entrepreneur working with disadvantaged children is Jeroo Billimoria, a serial social entrepreneur who has launched and brought to scale a number of transformational leveraged nonprofit enterprises. One of her first major efforts was the Childline India Foundation, a twenty-four-hour hotline for children in distress that now operates in seventy of India's largest cities. Building on this success, Billimoria founded Child Helpline International, which supported helplines in seventy-four countries in 2005—aiming for a hundred countries by 2007.

On the aging front, take Rick Surpin, who has founded three organizations—Cooperative Home Care Associates (CHCA) and its affiliated organizations, the Paraprofessional Healthcare Institute (PHI) and Independence Care System (ICS)—to help transform home health care in the United States. In so doing, Surpin has affected the labor supply available to the health care system and has also improved the lives of consumers in the system. There is plenty of competition in this space, but CHCA, founded in 1985, was the first worker-owned U.S. home health care agency. Its owner-employees are African American and Latina women, 70 percent of whom previously depended on welfare. Today, CHCA, a social business since its inception, has over a thousand workers and earns $25 million in revenues.

But it is ICS that has taken off as a model 3 business that serves Medicaid patients' previously unmet needs. When the organization started operations in 2000, it struggled. The first three years, it lost $1 million annually. Today, its annual revenue totals $70 million, and in two years, it projects that it will be at $120 million. ICS members are adults with physical disabilities because of neurological and muscular disease or injury, with a predominance of spinal cord injury and multiple sclerosis. All ICS members must be at least eighteen years of age, eligible for both Medicaid and placement in a nursing home. Only 10 percent of ICS members are white, 60 percent are women, and only 10 percent are over sixty-five years old. Today, ICS is establishing new offices in the Bronx, Harlem, Brooklyn, and other areas of New York.

Surpin says his biggest challenge is not financial; it is finding the right talent. He has managers, but they have a difficult time working in an organization that is, in his words, "constantly changing and always will."[3] Managers like structure, and it is hard for those whom Surpin has recruited to realize that adhering to structure is not the main purpose of an organization; growth creates new needs. "A lot of the tools that took us to where we are today," Surpin notes, "will not take us to where we want to be."

Ask him what business can learn from CHCA, PHI, and ICS, and Surpin reflects, "Our experience shows that a successful business model can treat direct service care workers and consumers—in our case, adults with physical disabilities—as key stakeholders, not just as sources of cost or revenue. Direct service care workers need quality jobs and are essential for providing quality services and care but are too often treated as replaceable parts. Adults with physical disabilities—the consumer, in our case—need individualized support to live independently but are usually treated as problems that will eventually go away."

Any business leader, mainstream entrepreneur, or investor thinking of taking on base-of-the-pyramid markets would be well advised to look at the business models organizations like Surpin's are adopting and adapting in the less privileged parts of the world's wealthier regions. In the process, they can tap into firsthand experience of the nature and scale of the second great divide that threatens the future.

Financial Opportunities

The notion that the haves will find ways to gain more and that the have-nots will lose more has been acknowledged since biblical times. But the already staggering divides in financial wealth have become even more dramatic in recent years as globalization and the spread of capitalism have skewed earnings and assets in many countries. In the United States, for example, the divide between rich and poor has been growing. By 2003, the top 1 percent of households owned 57.5 percent of corporate wealth, up from 53.4 percent a year before.[4] And China, which now has tens of thousands of multimillionaires, is going through its own age of robber barons.[5]

For many business—and political—leaders, this is the way of the world, particularly of the capitalist world, but extreme financial inequality can sow the seeds of insurrections and social cataclysms. So deep-seated are these drivers of economic injustice that entire societies have often had to be recalibrated by rebellions or revolutions. Where a suitable public policy context exists, governments can use taxation and related forms of wealth redistribution to address the financial divide. But where the tools and frameworks for economic justice are weak or nonexistent, entrepreneurs have much to offer in ensuring that—at worst—the divides do not grow further. Financial divides offer real opportunities to make things better for particular populations and groups.

Consider how the work of Childline's Jeroo Billimoria has evolved since 1995. Not content with simply bailing out children in distress, Billimoria has embarked on a new effort to break the cycle of poverty by teaching children about their rights and responsibilities—specifically, how to deal with money—and empowering them. This initiative was originally called Child Savings International and is now branded Aflatoun, which in India is a colloquial term used to refer to an intelligent, adventurous person who is not afraid to be different or to speak up. This is a model 1 venture, with strong ambitions to morph into a model 2. The concept was developed and tested in India before being rolled out in more than a dozen developing countries. The hope is that it can be replicated by franchising the model and branding to banks and other financial institutions internationally—in the process, generating a strong, ongoing source of revenues.

Billimoria suggests that the implications of Aflatoun's work for mainstream business is this: "Business needs to be agile, able to take quick, participatory decisions. Then, apart from the obvious issues of cost-effectiveness, accountability, and transparency, our experience shows that there is huge strength in diverse teams—drawn . . . from different cultural backgrounds, from different sectors (for example, civil society, government, and business), and from different levels of society."[6]

Another model 2 enterprise that has something of a head start in this space is KickStart, whose wild ambition is to help bridge the wealth divides by stimulating the growth of an entrepreneurial sector and, as a result, to create an African middle class. The organization seems well on its way to helping such countries as Kenya and Tanzania attain this goal. It creates new businesses and jobs by developing and promoting new low-cost technologies, which are bought and used by local entrepreneurs to establish profitable small-scale businesses. By identifying, developing, and marketing technologies with a high cost-benefit ratio, KickStart helps the entrepreneurial poor play an effective role in the market economy, substantially increasing their income levels and helping create jobs for others.

KickStart's success in selling its technology often raises the question of why it has not morphed into a model 3 venture. After all, its income revenue stream is substantial and growing. But KickStart's hybrid nonprofit status is the result of market failure. In the rich world, governments generally subsidize research and development to promote new technologies; governments in developing countries typically have other priorities and spend very little in this area. Private sector companies in these developing countries, meanwhile, rarely create new products and technologies for the poor, who have minimal purchasing power. To address this market failure, KickStart develops innovative, appropriate, and affordable machinery that people can use to start and increase the efficiency of small businesses in rural Africa. It uses its grant income to subsidize the research and development process that no company or government will undertake, and the resulting impact is huge. By the end of 2007, KickStart equipment had been used to create fifty thousand new small enterprises, with more than eight hundred new businesses created each month. These businesses generate nearly $452 million annually in new profits and wages and employ over thirty-five thousand people. The farmers purchasing KickStart technology today are the John Deere and Caterpillar consumers of tomorrow. This fact has not been lost on John Deere; the company has partnered with KickStart to help accelerate that trend.

Amazingly, it is estimated that KickStart's activities now generate over 0.6 percent of Kenya's GDP and 0.25 percent of GDP in Tanzania. This really should be a case taught in business schools worldwide—it can offer much suitable case material and many lessons to the rising generations of mainstream business executives.

On an even larger scale, consider the work of Fazle Abed in Bangladesh. He founded BRAC—the former Bangladesh Rural Advancement Committee—to fight poverty, illiteracy, and child mortality and to support women's health and development on a massive scale. His organization mobilizes the latent capacity of the poor to improve their own lives through self-organization. BRAC's full-time staff of over forty-five thousand has helped 3.8 million poor women establish a hundred thousand village organizations. BRAC now has over 5 million members in more than 180,000 village organizations across Bangladesh. In the process, BRAC identified "backward" and "forward" market linkages needed to boost economic opportunities for the poor. For example, when it found that poor women were not profiting from rearing dairy cows, it improved the breed of cow (a backward link) and set up a modern dairy (a forward link). In a prototypical case of the power of shifting the focus from risk and citizens' rights to opportunity and self-improvement, BRAC helped change the global development paradigm from that of helping "needy beneficiaries" to encouraging villagers', particularly women's, self-development.

When asked what mainstream business might learn from his experience, Fazle Abed says, "Poor people's livelihood opportunities tend to be constrained by market failures. It is a pity that business supply chains do not extend to them either as producers or consumers. BRAC's experience proves, however, that profitable enterprises can be initiated that expand the opportunities for the poor."[7] While it would be misleading to suggest that such impressive market positionings can be built in short order, or in time-frames that western capital markets are likely to be comfortable with, such organizations now have a huge reservoir of knowledge and experience in identifying and evolving base-of-the-pyramid markets for those with the appetite to take their businesses in this direction. The case of the joint venture between Danone and the Grameen Group, already covered in our introduction, is a striking example of how visionary business leaders and entrepreneurs are already driving into this space.

One lesson we draw from these cases is that the Henry Ford dream of jump-starting the creation of an entire middle class is alive and kicking in unimaginable places. Business leaders interested in developing long-term market positions in regions like East Africa, Asia, and South America would be well advised to seek out, engage with, and find ways to support such entrepreneurs. It may seem almost impossible to move the needle on something as big as a national economy, but people like Fazle Abed of BRAC and KickStart founders Martin Fisher and Nick Moon are demonstrating that it is well within reach of those able to dream big dreams and to develop the business models needed to turn those dreams into reality.

Nutritional Opportunities

The faces of the starving have helped catalyze major campaigns led by people like Mother Teresa, Bob Geldof, and Bono. True, famine, hunger, and poor nutrition have been constants throughout human history, but in today's interconnected world, the misery of others is visible as never before. At any time, it is estimated that over 800 million people around the world are hungry. In some cases, the root causes are outside people's control, as when natural disasters strike. But in others, as in a country like Zimbabwe, politics and human failings are at the root of the problem. In the process, hunger manifests itself in many ways other than starvation and famine.[8] Often forgotten is the fact that most poor people who battle hunger also deal with chronic undernourishment and vitamin or mineral deficiencies, resulting in stunted growth, weakness, and a greater susceptibility to illness. A considerable number of social entrepreneurs are tackling nutrition problems, either directly or indirectly. Let's take a quick look at examples from two very different Asian countries: Japan and Bangladesh.

In the next three decades, population growth and quality-of-life trends are expected to spur an estimated 70 percent increase in the demand for rice. Some people see that prospect as a huge commercial opportunity, but views on the nature, scale, and equity aspects of that opportunity vary. The Green Revolution—which increased food yields through intensive monocropping and the use of inorganic fertilizers, pesticides, and herbicides—is widely recognized today as unsustainable and environmentally unsound. Annual increases in the use of chemical fertilizers now often outstrip the growth of rice yields, lowering incomes and encouraging rural-to-urban migration. More and more farmers, caught in a trap of debt, have been committing suicide. Clearly, alternative systems are desperately needed.

That is where people like Takao Furuno come in. In the mid-1970s, this energetic Japanese farmer, who was influenced by Rachel Carson's book *Silent Spring*, decided to turn his farm organic. He spent ten years doing the backbreaking work of pulling out weeds by hand. Then, in a eureka moment in 1988, he stumbled across the traditional practice of using Aigamo ducks to protect rice. The ducks eat insects, pests, and snails. They also use their feet to dig up weeds—in the process, oxygenating the water and strengthening the roots of rice plants. It was a win-win solution. Furuno lovingly calls this method the "duck effect," and his farm yields have soared as a result of its use.

That is not all. Furuno has successfully marketed his "duck rice," which now sells at a 20 percent to 30 percent premium over conventionally grown rice in Japan and other countries. Today, his relatively small (3.2-hectare) farm provides an income of $160,000 a year from producing rice, organic vegetables, eggs, and ducklings. After demonstrating that small-scale organic farming can be highly productive, Furuno is now bent on disseminating his ideas. He has authored best-selling books, such as *The Power of Duck*, as well as an Aigamo duck cookbook. Through his writing, travel, lectures, and cooperation with agricultural organizations and governments, his methods have spread to more than seventy-five thousand farmers in China, Japan, Korea, Vietnam, the Philippines, Laos, Cambodia, and Malaysia.

Similar to Furuno, but in another part of the world, Mexico, entrepreneur Héctor González also used his know-how to come up with a new approach to addressing nutritional challenges. Unlike Furuno, however, González produced dairy products, having spent close to thirty years at the helm of Cuadritos, a successful milk, cheese, and yogurt company in the Mexican state of Guanajuato. As with most entrepreneurs, routine bored González. Once his company was established and doing well, he found himself looking for new ways to channel his energy. He was eager for something other than running Cuadritos and devoting his remaining time to race car driving. He wanted to do something for the thousands of Mexicans who suffer from severe malnutrition. He turned his sights to establishing a food bank, and in less than two years it became the largest self-sustaining food bank in Mexico, feeding 100,000 people a day. But even with this achievement under his belt, he was still restless. As he noted, "There are many food banks and our model was just more efficient, but it wasn't particularly innovative. I don't like to just copy models that have already proven to work—I like to do something different that no one has done before."[9]

And then he had an inspiration. What if he could turn the environmentally toxic (but protein-rich) "waste" resulting from cheese and yogurt production into products ready for human consumption? At that time, Cuadritos had developed a technology to dry this "waste," originally in the form of a thick liquid, so that it could be packaged and given free as pig feed to farmers. But perhaps there was a way to process that "waste" to elevate the nutritional levels of poor children and the elderly who were the hardest hit by protein deficiency?

According to his colleagues in charge of product research and development, González became obsessed with this project. After 15 months of working night and day, the team—enthused and driven forward by his vision—had transformed the reprocessed protein powder such that it was not only safe for human consumption, but also tasted good—and cost pennies to produce. Critically important, it also passed the consumer market test for taste and acceptability. Today, Cuadritos produces savory soups, biscuits, yogurts and soya milk based on this powder and distributes the products to major governmental and social organizations in charge of raising the nutritional level of Mexico's poor. González has designed an industrial plant that is capable of producing 3,500 tons of low cost, highly nutritious products. As the International Finance Corporation and the World Resources Institute note, this type of nutrient recycling could turn out to be the twenty-first century equivalent of the last century's push into areas like pulp and aluminum recycling.[10]

Recall that in comparison to their wealthier counterparts, the poor spend a much higher proportion of their income on food, limiting their capacity to educate and house their familias and protect their health. Entrepreneurs such as Furuno and González have come up with scalable ways to provide high quality nutrition to BOP markets, increasing their capacity to learn, work, play and—most fundamentally—seize opportunities to improve people's lives.

Resource Opportunities

A growing world population would not be a problem if the planet's resources were limitless, but they are not. Coupled with the global spread of resource-intensive agriculture and industry models, demographic pressures are fostering awareness of the natural resource limits to economic growth. In some places, the stresses are manifesting in periods of drought and starvation; in others, it's in the retreat of forests or the collapse of major fisheries. The challenge is further dramatized by the scramble for natural resources—such as oil, minerals, and timber—in regions like Africa, Latin America and the Arctic, as countries like China adopt similar economic and business models. The UN, for example, argues that the conflict in Darfur has been driven by competition for water as climate change bites. The prospects for making sense of all this may look bleak, but the reality is that huge opportunities abound here, too.

Scalable, entrepreneurial solutions need to be developed at all levels, helping track the trends and their impacts; ensuring full-cost pricing of resources; encouraging the transition to sustainable, renewable resources; and evolving and disseminating the necessary technologies. Energy may be the most obvious natural resource in short supply today, but others—among them, freshwater, ocean fish, and healthy urban air—are rapidly coming up the curve.

On the energy front, it is estimated that more than 2 billion people in developing countries do not have access to modern energy services and that 2.4 billion people rely on traditional (and often inadequate) biomass—derived from plant materials or animal waste—for basic energy needs. Such divides entrench poverty by limiting access to information, education, economic opportunities, and healthier livelihoods, particularly for women and children. They can also erode environmental sustainability at the local, national, and global levels. Systemic solutions to such challenges must involve political leadership and government action in such areas as taxation, resource pricing, and the planning and delivery of more efficient urban and industrial infrastructures. In the meantime, leading entrepreneurs are powering into the emerging opportunity spaces. Once again, a key characteristic is that they help others think differently.

Take Phil LaRocco, the human dynamo behind E+Co, a nonprofit company that has sponsored projects that now deliver energy to millions of people who would otherwise have had no access to its benefits.[11] Eric Usher, a UN clean-energy specialist, has noted that LaRocco has that rare ability to bring unlike people together in a common effort. "When he leaves the room," Usher explained, people tend to say, "'OK, this is on the edge of what we would normally consider, but let's give it a try.'"[12] How many companies and public sector agencies would benefit from looking beyond what they would normally consider?

LaRocco is not alone in this effort—or even in this field. Take Fabio Rosa, whose model 2 organization, Institute for the Development of Natural Energy and Sustainability (Ideaas), has pioneered systems to provide electricity to hundreds of thousands of impoverished rural Brazilians. As is the case with KickStart, Ideaas's hybrid nonprofit status reflects Rosa's need to subsidize research and development for new technologies. His widely replicated Palmares Project established the standard for low-cost electricity transmission in rural Brazil, reducing costs to consumers by more than 90 percent. Today, Rosa is spreading innovative "agro-electric" solutions that combine photo-voltaic solar energy, electric fencing and improved farming and grazing systems to simultaneously combat poverty, land degradation and global warming.[13]

Rosa is an excellent example of the need for social and environmental entrepreneurs to be able to transition between the public, private, and citizen sectors. As an agronomist and engineer, he began his work as a secretary of agriculture in Palmares do Sul, a rural municipality in Rio Grande do Sul, in southern Brazil. He found that 70 percent of rural dwellers lacked electricity. Because Brazil's electric distribution systems had been designed to serve large farms, factories, towns, and cities, high transmission costs placed electric service out of the reach of some 20 million rural Brazilians, exacerbating poverty and environmental destruction and intensifying rural-to-urban migration. Rosa sought to develop a more cost-effective approach to electricity distribution. To do so, he had to fight for years to get permission and cooperation from the federal and state governments, monopolistic power giants, bankers, mayors, equipment manufacturers, and even villagers likely to benefit.

His work also exemplifies the role of policy innovator that many social entrepreneurs assume to ensure both the sustainability and mass dissemination of their transformational efforts. In his case, he spent years battling with legislators to democratize energy provision and break the stranglehold held by Brazil's energy giants. He sought to allow smaller energy providers to offer off-grid energy provision (often of little interest to the larger companies). Finally, in 2003, he succeeded in getting the policy accepted at the federal level.

When quizzed about what business can learn from all this, Rosa replies:

> After twenty-plus years of hard-earned experience, I have come to the conclusion that business is too frequently hostage to its own corporate culture. It has great difficulty understanding what is occurring in its respective sectors and markets. Large national and multinational companies are hobbled by their sheer size and routine. They struggle to be innovative and flexible. And yet the moment to improve and change is now, introducing renewable energy and decentralized energy generation models that include providing energy to those who are excluded

from such services at prices they can afford to pay. In the field of energy, the revolution has already started and is being undertaken by smaller, entrepreneurial, and committed ventures, often without the participation of big energy companies and governments. There is a clear opportunity to change from [a] monopolistic energy market to a democratic energy market for everyone's benefit.[14]

The key point is that such people are showing that it is possible to provide natural-resource-based services in a cost-effective and sustainable fashion to people who, on the face of it, can scarcely afford to enter the twentieth century, let alone the twenty-first. If we can couple their work with the technological and scaling skills of companies like wind-power leaders Vestas and GE, the impact could jump to an altogether different level. Stand back for a moment, and it is clear that concerns about a growing range of environmental challenges, particularly climate change, will shift the energy issue into overdrive.

Environmental Opportunities

One of the most striking features of recent years has been the growing public concern about environmental issues and the greater interest in the green movement in general. Public opinion polls around the world have shown that ordinary citizens are waking up to the risks to their health, environment, and livelihoods posed by a range of problems, from poor urban air quality to droughts. And this is not simply a rich-world concern. The experts say there is no real north-south divide in caring for the environment: environmental concerns are universal, though different regions grapple with different problems.[15] Nevertheless, poor populations everywhere in the world are generally forced to live in the worst circumstances.

For most such people and communities, the dominant environmental concerns include the immediate necessities of clean water and sanitation, the risks of local and indoor pollution, and vulnerability to natural hazards. In wealthier parts of the world, by contrast, the hardest-felt problems may be noise, traffic congestion, air and water pollution, long-term climate change, and water shortages.

One way to get people to think about the really big environmental issues—particularly those that may impact people beyond the boundaries we choose to draw around our lives, nation states, or value chains—is to help them look at things from a different angle. One of the most successful entrepreneurs in this space has been Yann Arthus-Bertrand. He has produced a series of extraordinary books, exhibitions, and films that introduce people to the planet from the air—from a height where viewers often can see individual people going about their daily lives. Like all successful entrepreneurs, this aerial photographer has been virtually unstoppable. He shot over a hundred thousand images in compiling his extraordinary book *The Earth from the Air* alone. As one of his assistants put it, "With him, I learned that nothing is impossible. People will tell him 'No,' and he hears 'Maybe.' In the end he always gets what he wants." [16]

Another virtually unstoppable campaigner and entrepreneur has been Wangari Maathai, founder of Kenya's Green Belt Movement. Maathai is not simply interested in waking people up—she wants them to act. The first African woman to win the Nobel Peace Prize, Maathai won out against more than 190 other nominations— among them, Pope Paul II and UN weapons inspector Hans Blix. She founded the Green Belt Movement in her own backyard in 1977, aiming to plant trees to provide sustainable sources of firewood and to halt soil erosion, something that was already becoming a major problem. "In Kikuyu—my mother tongue—there's no word for *desert*," she explained, though as human pressures increase, previously fertile areas in Kenya are becoming parched and then desert.[17]

Like all successful campaigners and entrepreneurs, Maathai has a tough streak—one that showed when she came head-to-head with Kenya's then president Daniel Arap Moi. By 1989, Moi was an all-powerful figure in the country, a fact he wanted to underscore with a sixty-two-story skyscraper, topped with a sixty-foot statue of himself. Maathai was one of the most vociferous opponents of the scheme, arguing, "We owe billions to foreign banks. The people are starving. They need food, medicines and education. They do not need a skyscraper." Her stand incensed Moi and his regime, resulting in death threats that forced Maathai to take refuge with her three children in nearby Tanzania, though Moi ended up getting neither his skyscraper nor his statue. The personal toll that the exile took on Maathai was exacerbated by her divorce. Her husband claimed that she was "too educated, too strong, too successful, too stubborn and too hard to control." [18]

When Moi's reign was eventually brought to an end in 2002, Maathai won a parliamentary seat by a landslide. In short order, she became deputy environment minister. "Being a minister makes life easier," she later explained with a smile. "I'm able to educate my colleagues—the men have to take me seriously now." Getting into politics and government can also help leaders like Maathai, if they are minded to do so, change the market frameworks that shape the business case as seen by mainstream business and financial players. President Moi once described Maathai as a "wayward" woman, but the title of her autobiography used a different word, *unbowed*.[19] Wayward, unbound, unreasonable: Maathai's mind-set is displayed by many of the social entrepreneurs we spotlight, but her decision to enter the political realm is one that a growing number of mainstream innovators, entrepreneurs, and business leaders are following as they create and shape some of the new century's biggest markets.

Maathai and those like her are—in several senses—forces of nature. Business leaders keen to stay the course in the coming decades will need to seek such people out and work with them to understand how societal trends and market priorities are likely to change. Supporting such entrepreneurs will sometimes be seen as political by the powers that be, as was the support of certain business leaders for Nelson Mandela and the African National Congress party during South Africa's apartheid years. But these are calculated risks that courageous entrepreneurs and business leaders have always known how to take. By developing ongoing conversations with environmentalists and environmental scientists, moreover, business can work out how to boost early signals of impending challenges, and related opportunities, well ahead of the competition.

Health Opportunities

Health is a huge global business these days, but it is also another area where—from HIV/AIDS, to malaria, to potential pandemics like SARS—the problems can seem overwhelming. In 2005, the *World Health Report* concluded that in 2006 alone almost 11 million children under five years of age would die from largely preventable causes.[20] Among them, it was estimated, 4 million babies would not survive their first month of life. At the same time, it was thought that more than half a million women would die in pregnancy, during labor, or soon after childbirth.

Health issues are closely linked to many other factors already listed, including financial, nutritional, and environmental conditions. Climate change, for example, is estimated to be responsible for 2.4 percent of all cases of diarrhea worldwide and for 2 percent of all cases of malaria, and those figures are likely to increase as climate change accelerates.[21] At a time when major health care and pharmaceutical companies are under growing pressure to come up with preventative and curative medicines, they can learn a lot from the approaches and achievements of the current wave of social entrepreneurs. Many of the entrepreneurs already mentioned (like the Aravind Eye Care System in chapter 1) are also pursuing health improvements, directly or indirectly.

Anyone who questions the impact that one person can have on such issues should read Tracy Kidder's extraordinary book on the work of Dr. Paul Farmer in Haiti, Cuba, Peru, and Russia.[22] And someone who has had an equivalent impact is Mechai Viravaidya, the Thai Condom King discussed earlier, who expanded PDA's activities to include poverty reduction, HIV/AIDS, reproductive health, microcredit, environmental restoration, and democracy. In due course, the same groundbreaking approach applied to PDA helped build a comprehensive national HIV/AIDS prevention policy and program that is regarded as the most outstanding effort by any country in combating HIV/AIDS. By 2004, Thailand had experienced a 90 percent reduction in new infections. BRAC's health programs in Bangladesh, meanwhile, are reported to reach some 10 million people. The organization also pioneered oral rehydration therapy (for diarrheal disease), which played a major role in halving the country's infant mortality rate.

Meanwhile, in India, Dr. Devi Shetty has worked to make sophisticated health care available to all. A leading cardiologist, he founded Narayana Hrudayalaya in Bangalore at the dawn of the new millennium. It is a network of hospitals that provides 60 percent of treatments below cost or for free, thanks to reduced costs from high volumes and innovative management, plus donations. In our terms, it is a social business. In addition, a network of thirty-nine telephone centers reaches out to patients in remote rural areas. Two health insurance programs provide coverage for 2 million farmers at $4 per head per year.

Equally extraordinary is the work of Vera Cordeiro of Renascer, the hybrid nonprofit organization mentioned in chapter 2 that works to interrupt the cycle of child hospitalization in Brazil by reducing the effects of poverty that most contribute to repeat illness. Renascer mobilizes a wide network of volunteers to provide posthospitalization support to poor families of recently discharged children. Over a period of twelve months, customized assistance includes advice on nutrition, psychological counseling, vocational training, and housing improvements. As a result of its efforts, readmissions at the hospital where Renascer began the work have dropped by 60 percent, and the organization is now working to replicate its success throughout the country.

Ask Cordeiro what business can learn from her story, and she says:

As Stephan Schmidheiny, the founder of Avina, has noted, "There is no such thing as a successful company operating in a failed society." The health of a great proportion of the population living below the poverty line will only be improved through a huge collaborative and joint effort on the part of business, government, and civil society. Governments should use successful entrepreneurial efforts as the reference point to transform public policy. And if business wants to operate in a healthy society, a "marriage" needs to take place between companies and organizations of civil society, learning together how to serve the population. Business has much to share in this effort, providing organizations with tools and approaches, including technology, governance, resource mobilization, marketing and communications, and strategic planning. In this way, business and entrepreneurial organizations can be coauthors of a more just society that is healthy for all.[23]

And our take? Not only is the health sector an area where the issues of global demographics are likely to cause problems, but it is also one where we are likely to see new business models evolve and, in the process, leapfrog some aspects of western medicine. The fact that more westerners are now engaging in so-called medical tourism, visiting countries like India to take vacations and, as part of the same package deal, have surgery or undergo alternative therapies much more cheaply suggests the way things are heading.

Gender Opportunities

There is an inescapable gender component to all the issues mentioned so far—and to those that follow. Indeed, a range of gender divides has received attention in recent years. Disasters, for example, are rarely gender neutral. In the 1995 Kobe earthquake that hit Japan, one and a half times more women than men died.[24] In the 2004 Asian tsunami, death rates for women averaged three to four times those for men. Apart from men's and women's strength differences (e.g., when it comes to clinging to trees as a tsunami strikes), a number of other factors—biological, cultural, and economic—

come into play. These factors also turn out to influence other challenges, including access to health care, education, and information technology.

Struggling with such issues is virtually always an uphill task, even for those with considerable personal influence. Take Wu Qing, founder of the Beijing Cultural Development Center for Rural Women, a social enterprise in China that aims to improve the position of women and promote the status and public use of the law. Wu had a great start in life: her mother was China's most celebrated female author, and her father brought the study of sociology to China. Both were Chinese, studied in the best U.S. universities, and returned to their country to help people in desperate times. Even with such a background, however, Wu has had to fight to push China toward the rule of law and the empowerment of women.

To change China, she long ago concluded, the situation in rural areas must change, because China is primarily rural. And because women make up the majority of the inhabitants in such areas (many of their menfolk have moved to cities), changing women's mindsets is also crucial to changing the country. Wu, in fact, has been an advocate of women's rights in China for decades, having helped launch China's first university course on women's issues, in 1988. She also helped set up the first hotline to assist women in confronting problems of family, marriage, divorce, sexual harassment, and domestic violence.

Wu helped set up the *Rural Women Knowing All* magazine to raise awareness of the importance of encouraging women to develop their own potential and improve their health, knowledge of law, skills in different areas, and productivity. She has also been a legislator since 1984, elected for seven terms as the people's deputy to the Haidian district people's congress and for four terms to the Beijing municipal people's congress (the city parliament). In these capacities, she has worked long hours to hear the concerns of her constituents, using the constitution to challenge the authorities. For Wu Qing, the "rule of law must override the rule of men."[25] Her courage and impact are unusual, but people like her are crucial role models both in their own countries and—via the media, the Internet, and entrepreneur-linking networks—internationally. Given the scale of the oppression of women worldwide, this may be a vast opportunity space.

In our typology, the Beijing Cultural Development Center is a leveraged nonprofit venture (model 1), with funding initially coming from international sources, including the Ford Foundation, but more recently from the Chinese government. This is what Wu Qing thinks business can learn from her organization: "It is simple, really. We are all human beings first, women and men second. It is vital for women and men with gender awareness to work together and turn this imbalanced world into a world where women and men . . . not only [are] equal in terms of law but also enjoy equal opportunities across the board. To achieve this, we need people with a deep love for social justice, gender equality, and peace— and who are willing to take action. We have to be well prepared in terms of time, strategy, and a willingness to sacrifice. It is an uphill fight, but it will be worth it."[26]

Experience suggests that closed regimes eventually become more open and that, over time, the role of women becomes more critical in determining an evolving economy's health. As China ages, the gender effects of its long-standing one-child policy are likely to necessitate bringing women into the economic mainstream, a trend that western economies experienced during world wars and, more recently, as the service economy grew. The question for business is this: do we lean into this emerging future or try to turn a blind eye to it?

Educational Opportunities

As people like China's Wu Qing recognized long ago, few factors are as powerful as education in addressing all these great divides. Educational divides emerge and grow for many reasons, but as the processes of wealth creation become increasingly dependent on information and knowledge, the divides within and between countries become more significant. Entrepreneurial attempts to address these divides range from the grassroots approaches of organizations like Barefoot College (chapter 1) and First Book (chapter 4) to ventures designed to democratize different forms of technology, as explained in chapter 5.

Even in the richest countries, educational divides are stark and, as a result, have been attracting the attention of some extraordinary social entrepreneurs. Wendy Kopp, for example, turned her senior thesis at Princeton into Teach For America, founded in 1990. She pursued potential funders relentlessly, traveled the country, knocked on high-level doors, and refused to start small. Determined to begin Teach For America with no less than five hundred college graduate recruits, she saw achieving this scale from the outset as the only way to gain the national profile necessary to inspire the most talented graduating seniors to *compete* to teach in low-income communities. Each year, Teach For America recruits and selects a corps of recent college graduates, trains them, places them as full-time paid teachers in urban and rural public schools, and coordinates a support network to help them succeed. In the organization's first sixteen years, nearly seventeen thousand people joined Teach For America. By 2006, forty-four hundred corps members were reaching nearly three hundred seventy-five thousand students in twenty-five disadvantaged urban and rural communities.

City Year, to take another U.S. example, was founded in 1988 by Michael Brown and Alan Khazei, then roommates at Harvard Law School. They felt strongly that young people could be a powerful resource for addressing America's most pressing issues. They built City Year, a leveraged nonprofit venture, on the belief that one person can make a real difference and with the vision that, one day, service will be a common expectation—and a real opportunity—for citizens around the world. This vision has stimulated a commitment from the federal and state governments; today, they represent a significant source of City Year's funding. In fact, in 1993, President Clinton applied the City Year model to create a national network of service organizations, and since then, City Year has received a good portion of its operating budget from AmeriCorps.

City Year has also benefited from significant corporate interest. Local and national businesses found City Year a great vehicle for stimulating their employees' community involvement and an ideal way to promote their brand. For example, Timberland, the outdoor gear company, has been closely connected to City Year since the nonprofit's inception, when Timberland CEO Jeff Swartz became an avid City Year supporter. Other companies—including Bank of America, Comcast, and MFS Investment Management—have also provided significant capital and human resources to City Year for pretty much the same reasons: brand enhancement and staff volunteer commitment. And there are thousands of individuals across the United States who donate money to City Year annually.

The organization's signature program, the City Year youth corps, unites young adults aged seventeen to twenty-four in a demanding year of full-time service during which they work in diverse teams to address societal needs, particularly in schools and neighborhoods. These young leaders put their idealism to work as tutors and mentors to schoolchildren, reclaiming public spaces and organizing after-school programs, school vacation camps, and civic engagement programs for students of all ages. More than eleven hundred corps members serve in sixteen sites across the United States and one in South Africa; and City Year has generated 13 million hours of service to communities, helped nearly nine hundred thousand children, and engaged nearly nine hundred thousand other citizens in service.

A fascinating example outside the United States is Javier González, from abcdespañol, a hybrid nonprofit venture that generates income through contracts with education departments and multilateral development organizations committed to education. Across Latin America, many students repeat grades because they fail to meet reading and math standards. Not only does this situation increase the cost of national education, but it also prevents students from living up to their potential. González came up with the idea for abcdespañol while playing dominoes with his students' parents. He realized that, although they could not read or write, the parents consistently beat him at the game by using deductive logic, memorization, inference, and other mental skills needed for learning to read. This observation led him to believe that a key cause of students' low reading skills and high course-repetition rates was the rote learning methods employed in Latin American schools. He decided to figure out how to apply the skills observed in the parents to teach reading, writing, and math.

González works directly with education authorities in many countries, sharing his domino-based methodology with a core team of national educators or people (not necessarily teachers) who are committed to their communities. Each one of them learns the approach to pass it on to others and create a solid group of trained people who will then spread the methodology to target communities. In this fashion, the system can reach thousands of people, teaching them to read and/or do math in three to four months. Rather than assuming a traditional authority-figure role, the teacher motivates the students, ensuring their smooth progress. Students focus on relating to others, sharing ideas, and seeking compromise. Using the teaching method, they broaden their ability to grasp the necessary written language and math skills while deepening their emotional intelligence and problem-solving skills.

The same strategy applies in working with adults. The method has been adapted for teaching Spanish, English, Portuguese, and four indigenous languages: K'iché, Mam, Kaqchikel, and Q'eqchi'. The system has played a significant role in reducing the illiteracy rate in some Central American countries. In Guatemala alone, illiteracy dropped from 60 percent to 30 percent from 1995 to 1999.

There is a huge opportunity to cross-pollinate all forms of education with the perspectives, experience, and business approaches of leading social and environmental entrepreneurs. Meanwhile, consider the meteoric rise of Net Impact. Started in 1993 by MBA students who wanted to use their business skills to both make money and achieve positive social change, Net Impact currently has over eleven thousand paying members. With more than 120 student and professional chapters on four continents in seventy-five cities and eighty business schools, a central office in San Francisco, and partnerships with leading for-profit and nonprofit organizations, this extraordinary social venture enables members to use business for social good in their graduate education, careers, and communities. In 2006, the Net Impact annual conference drew over sixteen hundred participants. At Harvard, the student-organized group that focuses on social entrepreneurship is now the largest on campus, boasting nine hundred graduate students.

The message for leaders—whether they are in the public or private sectors or work in civil society institutions—is that education will be a key part of the solution to all the challenges sketched in this chapter. What the successes of organizations like abcdespañol, City Year, Net Impact, and Teach For America demonstrate is that removing the barriers to learning can release a flood of energy and, in the process, lay the foundations for more sustainable future economies.

Digital Opportunities

Enthusiasts may talk of "growing up digital," but the IT revolution has created its own divides. Meanwhile, the impact of enterprises like Grameenphone has underscored the importance of new technologies like cell phones, computers, and Internet connections for people worldwide, whether rich or poor. Still, it is an astounding fact that more than 80 percent of people in the world have never heard a dial tone, let alone surfed the Web. Some argue that the gap between information haves and have-nots is closing; others say that it is widening. Former UN secretary-general Kofi Annan warned of the danger of excluding the world's poor from the information revolution. As he put it: "People lack many things: jobs, shelter, food, health care and drinkable water. Today, being cut off from basic telecommunications services is a hardship almost as acute as these other deprivations, and may indeed reduce the chances of finding remedies to them."[27]

Despite the momentum in this sector, even the most skilled entrepreneurs make mistakes along the way. As in other areas, such failures often contain the seeds of long-term success. In Brazil, for example, Rodrigo Baggio's initial idea was to set up a bulletin board on the Internet so that rich and poor children could join in debates and exchange ideas. This failed miserably, however, because poor children never participated in the discussions. They had no access to computers.

So, with the help of volunteers, Baggio started collecting used computers, mostly from small firms, and donating them to community centers and neighborhood associations in low-income areas. IT, Baggio realized, could be used not only to increase job opportunities for poor youth but also to broaden their minds, help them understand their reality, point them in new directions, and raise their self-esteem.

Baggio's Committee for Democracy in Information Technology is a nongovernmental, nonprofit organization that aims to foster the social inclusion of less privileged social groups by using information and communication technologies to encourage active citizenship. It works in low-income communities and with institutions that assist special-needs individuals including the physically and mentally disabled, the visually impaired, homeless children, prisoners, and indigenous populations.

The model is based on the concept of helping people help themselves—and it is now spreading to countries like the United States and the United Kingdom. Ask Baggio what advice he would give to mainstream businesspeople, based on his experience to date, and he replies: "People don't die of hunger in our cities. They die from lack of opportunities, and that leads them into a life of crime, violence, drug trafficking, and death. People need more than just food: they also want fun, art, and technology in their lives."[28]

The key point for mainstream businesses here is that their IT-enabled business strategies are going to struggle to engage people who are digitally disenfranchised. While many businesses may conclude that bridging this gap is a job for governments, other companies have decided that partnering with leading digital revolutionaries, such as Baggio, in emerging markets could help their longer-term business prospects. This is not an easy area, however, as Hewlett-Packard discovered in implementing its e-inclusion strategy from 2000 to 2005.[29] In this case, corporate convulsions got in the way—and the program was canceled when its business prospects didn't materialize fast enough to satisfy a new CEO and, ultimately, Wall Street.

Other companies have experienced similar difficulties in attempting to address the digital divide. But the technology gap is so great, and the potential opportunities so vast, that we will return to examine the subject more closely in chapter 5. Experience suggests that the adoption rate of modern computing and Internet-based learning and business methods puts the leverage potential of this opportunity area ahead of much of the pack as long as other needs—among them, safe water, nutritious food, and a secure supply of electricity—are met.

Security Opportunities

Bill Drayton's colleagues at Ashoka were horrified to see the hijacked American Airlines flight 77 smash into the Pentagon in 2001. One result of these attacks was that the United States and its allies went into overdrive to achieve greater levels of security. That, in turn, meant huge commercial opportunities for those offering such products and services as closed-circuit television cameras, retinal scanners, and body armor.

Although governments currently turn to companies like General Dynamics and Halliburton for security measures, perhaps they should turn instead to leading social and environmental entrepreneurs, who have very different views on what it will take to ensure real security in this century. These new leaders recognize and address physical, psychological, social, economic, energy-related, water-related, and environmental security, among other forms.

People like Takao Furuno, the duck rice entrepreneur, and Ibrahim Abouleish of Sekem (introduced in chapter 1), not only help boost farmers' incomes and decrease their workload but also reduce environmental damage and increase food security. Similar arguments can be made for all the entrepreneurs mentioned here, although the types of security they help ensure range over a big spectrum. Stepping back, however, it is clear that wider failures to address many key challenges—including poverty, hunger, disease, and environmental breakdown—undermine the security of countries and communities that seem remote from the problems. Yet rich western countries spend up to twenty-five times as much on defense as they do on overseas aid, according to UN figures.[30]

Mainstream leaders must learn these lessons fast. This next example may shock many readers, but just think of the way Hezbollah—particularly its civil-engineering arm, Construction Jihad—seized the initiative from the Israelis by rebuilding devastated parts of south Beirut after the 2006 war.[31] It's unlikely that Hezbollah will receive any of the social capitalist awards offered by magazines like *Fast Company*, but its use of social networks—based on schools, hospitals, and a banking system—is in many ways typical of an entrepreneurial approach in the public interest.

There are small signs of progress in the West. The aerospace giant Boeing, for example, has worked with Pioneer Human Services, alongside other corporate partners like Genie Industries, Nintendo, and Starbucks. Founded in 1963, Pioneer helps each year some fifteen thousand people from the margins of society find low-cost housing, overcome addictions, and secure employment after imprisonment. With an operating budget in the region of $60 million, this model 2 organization manages to help 80 percent of the unemployed people who turn to it find a job. And, significantly, Pioneer does not look for charitable contributions from the companies it partners with. Instead, its leaders insist that they "simply want the opportunity to compete for and win contracts to provide quality work and services."[32] Revenues are earned through the manufacture, distribution, and sale of products and through fees for services. "Less than one percent of the annual budget is derived from donations, contributions, or grants," Pioneer reports.[33]

In the big scheme of things, such partnerships are small stepping-stones. The point is that the global forms of security that major political leaders so obsess about cannot be achieved—or sustained—without successful large-scale efforts to address all the divides covered here. Indeed, as Muhammad Yunus insisted when accepting the Nobel Peace Prize, "Peace is inextricably linked to poverty." [34] More, he stressed, "Poverty is a threat to peace." He went on to say that our world's income distribution makes "a very telling story. Ninety-four percent of the world income goes to 40 percent of the population, while 60 percent of people live on only 6 percent of the world's income. Half of the world population lives on two dollars a day. Over one billion people live on less than a dollar a day. This is no formula for peace."

Then he got controversial. "The new millennium began with a great global dream," he recalled. "World leaders gathered at the United Nations in 2000 and adopted, among others, a historic goal to reduce poverty by half by 2015. Never in human history had such a bold goal been adopted by the entire world in one voice, one that specified time and size. But then came September 11 and the Iraq war, and suddenly the world became derailed from the pursuit of this dream, with the attention of world leaders shifting from the war on poverty to the war on terrorism." The problem, he argued, is that we have misunderstood what security is—and how it is best achieved. "I believe terrorism cannot be won over by military action," he added. "Terrorism must be condemned in the strongest language," but, he insisted, "putting resources into improving the lives of the poor people is a better strategy than spending it on guns."

Unfortunately, the evidence to date suggests that major corporations—especially those that serve the defense sector—fail to see both the wider security risks and the opportunities of bridging the great divides we have outlined, notably the poverty gap. We turn to that subject in chapter 4.

FOUR

Raising Expectations for Bonsai Consumers

UNREASONABLE ENTREPRENEURS find opportunity in the chasms that separate the fortunate from the not-so-fortunate. But to cross the great divides discussed in chapter 3, entrepreneurs must first understand—and then try to reshape—the thinking of those on the other side. Too often, the people who suffer most from deprivation have little reason to hope for a better future. If they are to rise out of a victim mind-set, they need to discover a sense of hope, a voice, and a will to act. To do so, they need a prospect of improving their living conditions.

Total equality will always be impossible, but inequity on the scale now seen around the world is likely to prove unsustainable in relatively short order and in a number of ways. That is why so many of the entrepreneurs in this book have set out to raise the expectations of the poorest of the poor.

These are the populations Muhammad Yunus described as "bonsai people" in his Nobel Prize acceptance speech: "To me poor people are like bonsai trees," he said. "When you plant the best seed of the tallest tree in a flower-pot, you get a replica of the tallest tree, only inches tall. There is nothing wrong with the seed you planted, only the soil-base that is too inadequate. Poor people are bonsai people. There is nothing wrong in their seeds. Simply, society never gave them the base to grow on. All it needs to get the poor people out of poverty is for us to create an enabling environment for them. Once the poor can unleash their energy and creativity, poverty will disappear very quickly."[1]

The academic community uses language less poetic than Yunus's, but an important body of research supports his message. Professors C. K. Prahalad and Stuart Hart, to name just two scholars, have written extensively about base-of-the-pyramid (BOP) markets and the power of partnering with the poor.[2] To get a sense of how social entrepreneurs are helping liberate the growing number of bonsai (or BOP) consumers from the constraints that rule their lives, we devote this chapter to three critical aspects of the challenge.

The first involves the issue of *access*, which we explore through the work of Victoria Hale and her Institute for OneWorld Health. Second, we investigate the prospect for radically cutting the *price* of products and services, spotlighting the work of such organizations as Aurolab and First Book. Finally, we turn to the question of *quality*, which we will examine through the lens offered by Nicholas Negroponte and One Laptop per Child, investigating organizations like Novatium and Recycla Chile along the way.

By addressing all three issues—access, price, and quality—together, these social and environmental entrepreneurs are seeding and growing significant new markets where none existed before. At best, their work creates a virtuous cycle of sustainability: access to better-quality products and services at prices affordable to a broader segment of the population generates consumer demand, which in turn increases volume and leads to further cost reductions.

Of course, none of these ventures is guaranteed success. Indeed, many will fail—but we must hope that they at least fail in interesting ways. In the process, they will broaden the thinking of new generations of innovators, entrepreneurs, businesspeople, investors, and governments (the last of which represents a crucial factor in ensuring that emerging solutions are broadly equitable and both economically and environmentally sustainable in the longer term). Just as important, such social ventures will help raise the expectations of those whose basic needs currently go unmet—and thus begin to seed the relevant markets of the future.

What's the message for business and public sector leaders in this chapter? Social and environmental entrepreneurs may blaze the trail, experimenting with new solutions and enduring the early failures that deter major players, but in the end, mainstream businesses will have to do some serious heavy lifting to replicate and scale the successful solutions. In short, these entrepreneurial projects are not alternatives to public and private sector action but early indicators of the seismic market developments soon to come.

Access: Attacking Neglected Diseases

Access is a troubling issue for mainstream businesses, particularly those in the pharmaceutical sector. Think of the way that the human rights agenda has mutated in recent years, from an initial concern with torture and political abuse to a concern with wider social, economic, and environmental rights. There have been growing calls for universal access to essentials like clean water, affordable energy, and medicines for HIV/AIDS, tuberculosis, and malaria. That's all well and good—unless your business model depends on long-term research, considerable investment, and early premium pricing, which are all wrapped around intellectual property rights.

One small spark of light for the pharmaceutical industry has been the work of Dr. Victoria Hale, recognized in 2002 as an outstanding social entrepreneur by the Schwab foundation. Since then, she has received multiple national and international awards, including the Social and Economic Innovation Award from *The Economist*, the Exec of the Year award from *Esquire*, and the Pharmaceutical

Achievement Award. As if that were not enough, she and her organization, the Institute for OneWorld Health, were given one of the MacArthur Foundation's coveted "genius grants" in 2006.

Such high visibility comes with a public health warning of its own. There are those who think that Hale and her work have been overexposed and overpraised by the media, a charge—it has to be said—that has been leveled at several other leading social entrepreneurs. But a few things are indisputable. Perhaps most important, OneWorld Health is considered to be the first nonprofit pharmaceutical company in the United States, and its mission and business model are highly unusual. Hale founded this model 1 company to develop new drugs for diseases that affect the world's poorest people. The business model involves two key ingredients: the institute's team of scientists uncovers promising drug candidates and ushers them through clinical trials and regulatory approval. Then, to ensure both affordability and sustainability, OneWorld Health contracts manufacturing and distribution to companies and organizations in the developing world—in the process, creating new paths to economic development.

With the specific goal of separating profitability from a drug's potential to cure disease, OneWorld Health leverages promising industry research to create life-saving medicines for those patients most in need. It has been estimated that only 10 percent of global spending on health is devoted to diseases or conditions that account for 90 percent of the global disease burden. Strikingly, of the approximately fifteen hundred new drugs approved in the past twenty-five years, fewer than twenty were for so-called neglected infectious diseases that disproportionately affect the poor.

Most of these diseases are unheard of in industrialized countries. They include leishmaniasis, schistosomiasis, onchocerciasis, African sleeping sickness, lymphatic filariasis, and Chagas disease. Others, such as diarrheal disease, are ubiquitous, but their impact is severest in the developing world: 2 million children under age five die each year from diarrhea, and more than 1 million people die each year from malaria, most of them children as well. Meanwhile, numerous potential cures exist but remain undeveloped.

OneWorld Health aims to correct this unacceptable market failure. The institute's business model offers pharmaceutical companies and universities an entity through which to share and/or donate intellectual property, lend professional experts, or make financial contributions. This enhances companies' and universities' role in promoting global health and allows them to receive credit for their support.

Hale explains the process as follows: "Many, many pharmaceutical professionals want to contribute to developing a new medicine, particularly a cure, for a deadly disease. We all are well aware that the poorest among us have the greatest needs for new medicines. There was simply no place for such professionals to gather to work together; there was no vehicle suitable to accept donated intellectual property. With a nonprofit company, the expertise, the technologies, and the funding are garnered and advanced to save lives of people who were forgotten."[3]

This new paradigm for global health encourages collaboration and has the potential to shave years and millions of dollars off the traditional development path for new drugs. But what does this mean in practice? OneWorld Health's first late-stage drug development program has involved an off-patent antibiotic that was no longer manufactured to treat visceral leishmaniasis, the second-deadliest parasitic disease after malaria, because it was not profitable. Yet this is a disease that in recent times has produced more than half a million new cases annually on three continents. OneWorld Health completed phase 3 clinical trial and subsequently obtained approval to use the medicine in India in 2006. In addition, it leads a malaria drug program and is building a portfolio of new drugs for diarrheal disease with a special focus on treatments for children.

If Hale is unwilling to pursue profits, where does she obtain her financing? Foundation and government funding is key. Significant funding for OneWorld Health has come from the Bill & Melinda Gates Foundation. The organization has also received royalty-free intellectual property donations from industry and academia and has benefited immensely from the intellectual contributions of hundreds of pharmaceutical scientists and business professionals who have rallied to support its mission.

If you ask Hale about the main challenges she faces in bringing OneWorld's products to market, she replies, "The greatest challenge has been a bit of a surprise to us technologists: how to deliver new medicines to the people and [get them to] use the medicines correctly. Inevitably, it is the poorest people who often live very remotely that suffer and die from curable diseases. Though we are a pharmaceutical company, we do not have a sales and marketing force. Our patients are practically invisible to global enterprises. In this case, we rely on local entrepreneurs and rural health care providers. Many of these individuals are social entrepreneurs. We need to recognize that we are all just one link in a chain that is essential to have impact and change the world."

Price: Slashing Costs by 90 Percent

Providing access to things people need is one thing, but ensuring that the price is right tends to be a different challenge. Some people are willing—and able—to pay almost any price for life-saving drugs, but for most people, cost is a crucial consideration in determining what products they can use, even if those products are easily accessible. So, whether or not social entrepreneurs articulate it this way, slashing the price of key western products and services by around 90 percent has become their ultimate goal.

This, as explained in chapter 3, is something that Fabio Rosa has already done with electricity in Brazil. His widely replicated Palmares Project established the standard for low-cost electricity transmission in rural Brazil, reducing costs to consumers by more than 90 percent. Rosa, however, is not alone.

David Green and Aurolab

David Green established Aurolab, a model 2 manufacturing facility in South India in 1992. Green has developed an economic paradigm for making health care products and services available and affordable to the poor. His philosophy of "compassionate capitalism" uses excess production capacity and surplus revenue to serve all economic strata, rich and poor alike.

Aurolab has grown to be one of the largest manufacturers of intraocular lenses in the world, with over 5 million lenses sold in more than 109 countries. The lenses are surgically implanted in the eye to replace a cloudy, cataract-damaged lens. (Cataract disease is the main cause of blindness and visual disability in the world.) Aurolab sells for $2 to $4 lenses that are priced at $150 in the developed world, thereby helping countless patients who otherwise could never afford such treatment to preserve their sight and ability to work.

Mainstream intraocular lens companies selling approximately the same volume of lenses as Aurolab have a hundred times the revenue. Yet not only is Aurolab able to serve 10 percent of the global market; it has also achieved both product affordability for its customers and economic sustainability for itself by carefully tailoring its costs and margins.

This is what Green has to say about the main challenges he faces in bringing such products to market:

> The first challenge is finding R&D people to work with who know about the technology in question and who are willing to share their knowledge. These are usually individuals and not companies, since companies are generally unwilling to share for all the obvious reasons. The second challenge is developing a product development process that does not infringe intellectual property or violate trade secrets but still results in state-of-the-art [treatments] for the poor. The third challenge is getting the product into affordable manufacturing. The fourth and perhaps greatest challenge is marketing and distribution: developing unconventional distribution which minimizes margins and which enables [Aurolab to reach] the intended beneficiaries is quite challenging. The final challenge is being properly capitalized to enact all the steps, particularly for developing distribution.[4]

As he addresses all these challenges, Green stresses the importance of finding new ways to measure value when working with mainstream partners. Ventures like Aurolab, he notes, need "to work with a strong partner that has ethical fiber and perseverance for maximizing distribution over maximizing return on investment to shareholders."

Green also helped develop India's Aravind Eye Care System (profiled in chapter 1), which performs 250,000 surgeries per year, making it the largest eye care system in the world. Seventy percent of the care is provided free of charge or below cost, yet Aravind's hospitals are able to generate substantial surplus revenue. Green has replicated this cost-recovery model in countries like Nepal, Malawi, Egypt, Guatemala, Tibet, Tanzania, and Kenya.

Another focus area for Aurolab is suture manufacturing. The company has cut the price of ophthalmic sutures from $200 per box to $30. Previously, only 10 percent of suture products were sold to developing countries, where 70 percent of the world's population lives. As a serial entrepreneur, Green has also led Aurolab to manufacture a low-cost, digitally programmable analog hearing aid that uses solar power to charge batteries. An estimated 250 million people could benefit from hearing aids, yet only 6 million are sold each year, mostly in developed countries. The device, normally priced at $1,500, is now manufactured at a cost of $50 and is priced for poor customers on a sliding scale from free of charge to $200.

Ask Green what mainstream business and public sector leaders could learn from Aurolab's example, and he suggests:

> For every product development cycle, we start out with the assumption that things don't really cost that much to make. We demystify cost structure and the technology and develop manufacturing where our cost structure is no different from major western companies. The truth is, the emperor really is not wearing any clothes—it doesn't really cost that much to make ostensibly sophisticated medical devices. Most companies could have a

manufacturing cost structure and sufficient production capacity to profitably serve the needs of lower-income countries, but they don't. I believe there's a way for these companies to price their products to be affordable for developing country markets in ways that don't jeopardize profitability in higher-margin developed country markets. My life would be much easier if I could just convince these companies to seriously look at developing the higher-volume, lower-margin developing country markets with their present product lines. This would save me a lot of hassle in manufacturing and becoming their competitor.

Kyle Zimmer and First Book

Such ventures are not confined to developing countries. Let's turn to a case that powerfully underscores the fact that bonsai and BOP markets are everywhere, even in the most basic information technology: the book. Kyle Zimmer, founder of First Book, experienced her epiphany while working at a community-based center in downtown Washington, D.C., home to many African American and Latino families and starkly different from the surrounding wealthy neighborhoods and affluent suburbs. There she worked as a volunteer tutor to youngsters in early-childhood programs.

"It opened my eyes," Zimmer recalls. "The program where I volunteered is a relatively well-funded institution as these kinds of institutions go. But as I browsed through the reading materials available to those children, I was appalled. They were really poor."[5] She began "reading studies and nosing around," as she puts it, trying to find out what was going on in Washington, D.C., and other cities. "What I found," she says, "was a gigantic chasm." Children had no books. When she dug deeper, she discovered that the majority of low-income families in the United States have no age-appropriate books for their children. In fact, the absurd truth, uncovered in a University of Michigan study, was that randomly selected middle-income households had approximately thirteen books per child and that low-income neighborhoods had one book for every three hundred children.[6]

An attorney by trade, Zimmer says she put her private sector head to work and thought of Henry Ford and the Model T: if you want to put a car in everyone's driveway, or a book in every house, you need to price it right. Next, you need to have an assembly line in place that allows you to get as many books to as many low-income children as possible. So that is what she set out to do. With two other lawyers, Peter F. Gold and Elizabeth Arky, she founded First Book in 1992, as a hybrid nonprofit (model 2).

First Book's early mission was simple: give children from low-income families the opportunity to read and own their first new books. It began in three communities and distributed twelve thousand books in the first year. By May 2007, the organization had celebrated the distribution of more than 48 million books through a network of over three thousand communities across the United States. First Book has also begun operations in Canada and taken early steps in India, where support is building with NGOs, foundations, and individuals, including senior members of the Indian government.

An evaluation by Louis Harris & Associates found that when First Book works with a local organization serving the most disadvantaged children, the number of children who previously had "low interest" in reading fell dramatically from 43 percent to 15 percent and those with a "high interest" in reading more than doubled, from 26 percent to 55 percent.[7] Moreover, 92 percent of children stated that they "love" receiving books they can call their own and take home, and 80 percent noted that "it means a lot to receive something new and not used." Most important, 69 percent of children reported a marked improvement in their interest in reading: 63 percent are "not unhappy to have to take time away from play to read," and 80 percent "really like to read books on their own."

If ever there was a BOP opportunity, it was here, and by the early 2000s, Zimmer and her partners began to think about setting up a model 3 for-profit outlet to complement First Book. By creating the First Book Marketplace (FBMP), they hoped to offer a broad selection of high-quality, relevant children's books in unlimited quantities at a price far below what was then available to programs serving disadvantaged children. Moreover, FBMP would do this through a user-friendly online ordering process with no complex procedures. And First Book could use the revenues generated from FBMP to scale up the original operation so that more low-income children could get free books.

As a reality check on the plan's feasibility, First Book began by conducting a survey of ten thousand programs focused on low-income children. Would they be willing and able to pay something for the books? Yes, it seemed they would: of the organizations surveyed, 68 percent had money to purchase low-cost new children's books. Even better, the two hundred thousand to three hundred thousand programs serving children from low-income families in the United States have an annual estimated book-buying power of at least $86 million. So, in 2004, the group quietly launched a FBMP pilot, which in two years had generated sales of over $1 million for five hundred fifty-five thousand books to more than eight hundred programs.

Since then, the numbers have continued to climb. As of 2007, more than twenty thousand programs had signed up to become part of the First Book system—a fourfold increase in under two years—and sales revenues were on track to more than double those of the previous year.

FBMP's social business works like this: First Book purchases selected inventory and customized reprints from publishers in carton quantities on a nonreturnable basis. Books available for purchase are then posted on the FBMP Web site. Inventory is stored using the donated warehouse space already provided to First Book. Customer programs register and order through a simple online system. The price per book averages $1.80, including shipping and handling, and generates a margin of $0.75 for FBMP. The icing on the cake, at least for the publishers, is that they are able to guarantee that they will have no return books, but the real impact is found in the minds of children.

Zimmer has this to say about what mainstream business and public sector leaders could learn from First Book's story: "There is nothing new under the sun. We have been able to take the best practices regarding market aggregation from the private sector and leverage those models with the unique advantages of a social enterprise. These hybrid strategies certainly have broader applications."

Does she worry about competition entering First Book's markets? She replies, "We feel very confident of our ability to compete in the marketplace, but First Book is fundamentally a mission-focused organization. If the result of increased competition is that books become more accessible to children in need, then we have accomplished our goal."

Quality: Targeting the $100 Laptop

If a book is a window into a different world, how much more so is a laptop connected to the Internet? But to open such a window for BOP markets, entrepreneurs need to consider the relationship between cost and quality—the third key element of the success equation. Many western products—among them, computers—are overengineered for their actual purpose, which drives up costs and puts much-needed products even further out of reach of poor people, wherever they live. E. F. Schumacher, in his seminal 1973 book *Small Is Beautiful: Economics as if People Mattered*, argued instead for what he called "appropriate technology" suited to real needs in developing countries and emerging economies.[8]

Nicholas Negroponte and One Laptop per Child

One striking example of rethinking product design to achieve radical cost reductions places the spotlight on Nicholas Negroponte, chairman of One Laptop per Child (OLPC) and author of books like *Being Digital*.[9] His quest? To produce a laptop computer that would be affordable for much larger numbers of people worldwide, particularly young people, and that would be designed from the bottom up (as opposed to being just a cost-down version of other laptops). The target price? An almost-inconceivable $100. By 2007, Negroponte had achieved a $170 prototype, but he was determined to hit his $100 target by the end of 2009.

After a few early iterations, the prototype design looked great by early 2007. At that year's World Economic Forum summit in Switzerland, there were queues of people waiting to use the dozen or so machines on display. Designed to be run on Linux (but able to run Windows as well), the laptop has both a full-color mode and a black-and-white, sunlight-readable display option. Although the laptop will have a 800 MHz processor and 256 MB of DRAM, with 1 GB of Flash memory, it will not have a hard drive.

"The laptops will have wireless broadband that, among other things, allows them to work as a mesh network," Negroponte explains. "Each laptop is able to talk to its nearest neighbors, creating an ad hoc, local area network. The laptops will use innovative power sources and be able to do most everything except store huge amounts of data."[10] And, he adds, "It also happens to be the greenest laptop ever built, by as much as an order of magnitude."[11] Push him, though, and he accepts that this was a side effect of the design, rather than an intended outcome.

Laptops, Negroponte continues, "are both a window and a tool: a window into the world and a tool . . . with which to think. They are a wonderful way for all children to *learn learning* through independent interaction and exploration." But why not use a desktop computer—or, even better, the sort of recycled computer that social entrepreneurs like Rodrigo Baggio of Committee for Democracy in Information Technology are collecting, refurbishing, and offering? "Desktops are cheaper," Negroponte agrees, "but mobility is important, especially with regard to taking the computer home at night. Kids in the developing world need the newest technology, especially really rugged hardware and innovative software."

Recent work with schools in Maine, he says, has shown the huge value of using a laptop across all of a child's studies, as well as for play. "Bringing the laptop home engages the family," he notes. "In one Cambodian village where we have been working, there is no electricity, thus the laptop is, among other things, the brightest light source in the home. Finally," he adds, "regarding recycled machines: if we estimate 100 million available used desktops, and each one requires only one hour of human attention to refurbish, reload, and handle, that is forty-five thousand work years. Thus, while we definitely encourage the recycling of used computers, it is not the solution for One Laptop per Child."

So how have Negroponte and his team cut costs so radically, and what is hindering their ultimate target of the $100 computer? Negroponte is happy to explain how they plan to crack the challenges:

> First, by dramatically lowering the cost of the display. The first-generation machine will have a novel, dual-mode display that represents a major industry innovation that is certain to find itself in other products. These displays can be used in high-resolution black and white in bright sunlight—all at a cost of approximately $40. Second, we will get the fat out of the systems. Today's laptops have become obese. Two-thirds of their software is used to manage the other third, which mostly does the same functions nine different ways. Third, we will market the laptops in very large numbers (millions), directly to ministries of education, which can distribute them like textbooks.

And how is the production side being handled? The machines are to be made by Quanta Computer Inc. of Taiwan, the world's largest manufacturer of laptop PCs. Equally encouraging are the names that are backing the OLPC venture. In addition to several faculty members from the MIT Media Lab, the list of founding members includes such corporations as AMD, Brightstar, Chi Mei, Citigroup, eBay, Google, Marvell, News Corp., Nortel, Red Hat, and SES Astra. Negroponte underscores one key strength of the OLPC model: "Sales, marketing, distribution, and profit represent over 50 percent of the cost of any laptop. OLPC has none of those."[12]

Some of these partner companies view OLPC as a highly leveraged form of corporate philanthropy, but others see the venture as the thin end of a wedge into tomorrow's markets. Certainly, Negroponte's ambitions are breathtaking. If things go according to plan, OLPC will be shipping at least 50 million machines a year by the end of 2009, more than all the laptops sold worldwide in 2005. The initial price will be closer to $150 but is projected to drop to $100 as economies of scale take effect. Perhaps the key point here is that such ultra-low-cost projects have the potential not only to meet the needs of some of the world's poorest but also to leapfrog back into rich-world markets as a complete new category of disruptive products.

There may be, however, a number of flies in the ointment. One issue raised by teachers and government officials in countries like India is whether children would be better serviced learning together rather than disappearing into their own worlds, courtesy of their laptops. In the United States, some communities have been dropping their free laptop programs, concerned that young people have been using their machines for games and surfing rather than more educational pursuits. But this doesn't have to be an either-or discussion. Children can learn together *and* use computers to continue the process on their own, as long as their cultural environment promotes learning and has the means to check how these extraordinary tools are being used.

Another risk to the project is that someone else may come along with a different—even cheaper—idea. For example, Rajesh Jain's Novatium intends to exploit the fact that many Indian homes have TVs to create PC-lite systems, able to access the Internet for as little as $70.[13] Negroponte says he is unfazed by the risk of competition. "We no more compete with vendors than the Red Cross competes with Johnson & Johnson," he says. "The more options, the better. Can OLPC stop making its laptop? No. If we do, the prices will go back up. Ours will keep going down."[14] But here is an uncomfortable paradox: sometimes, entrepreneurs will open up market opportunity spaces that others will be better equipped to move into.

Fernando Nilo and Recycla Chile

Then there is the nagging question of what to do with all the result-ing electronic waste, or "e-waste," from these laptops. Although computers—as well as televisions, mobile phones, fax machines, and scanners—are indispensable modern technologies, when they out-live their usefulness and need to be disposed of, they can be highly toxic for the environment unless discarded properly. The ability to address the end of the product life cycle in ways that achieve eco-nomic efficiency, social practicality, and environmental quality will be key—and possibly the origin of other as-yet-unimagined markets.

One social entrepreneur who is addressing the e-waste challenge is Chile's Fernando Nilo, founder of Recycla Chile. Until recently, Recycla Chile was the only company in Latin America that recycled e-waste. Nilo recognized the e-waste problem as a major business op-portunity, though at the forefront of his concern was social and envi-ronmental transformation. To achieve the former, he established a system whereby the personnel at Recycla Chile who dismantle the electronic appliances and consolidate the parts for export are former prison inmates who want to reintegrate into the workplace and soci-ety. To achieve the latter, perhaps a more difficult task, Nilo has em-barked on a massive campaign to raise awareness, both in his country and beyond, of the urgent need to recycle e-waste—a process that will also require changes in public policy. To date, for example, there is no Chilean legislation that makes recycling mandatory.

Despite these challenges, Recycla Chile, which is a social busi-ness, has begun to make a profit. From modest origins in 2003, its annual budget reached $3 million by 2007. Revenues have contin-ued to grow almost exponentially as enlightened companies hire Recycla Chile to collect and dismantle their e-waste. Recycla Chile then exports the raw material to European companies that specialize in e-waste reprocessing or disposal. Recycla Chile also receives and dismantles computers for other social organizations at no cost.

Access, price, and quality are all likely to be critical determinants of whether particular solutions targeted to BOP markets will take flight. The work of ventures like Aurolab, OLPC, OneWorld Health, and Recycla Chile are just some of the social and environmental enterprises now working to create the technological solutions of a more equitable and sustainable future. Their efforts to bridge the great divides we face are so ambitious and yet so necessary—from today's perspective, so powerfully unreasonable—that we'll spend the next chapter digging deeper into the relevant risks and opportunities.

Part III

Leading Sustainable and Scalable Change

FIVE

Democratizing Technology

CAN YOU PICTURE Mahatma Gandhi toting a video camera to expose human rights abuses, flying a jet plane to ship in relief supplies to devastated communities, or genetically engineering a crop plant to provide more nutritious foods for the hungry? Probably not, but for many social entrepreneurs, Gandhi has been a life-long inspiration, their beacon and navigational reference point. Not only did he promote self-sufficiency with his goats and spinning wheels, but he also helped catalyze systemwide change. He shook the British Raj to its roots with his astonishing march to the sea to boil salt, evading the much-hated salt tax. Today, a growing number of social entrepreneurs carry his torch, but many do so using technologies he would have found incredible.

One Laptop per Child, the ambitious venture we profiled in chapter 4, embraces technology to create the markets of the future. We cannot rely on technical fixes to solve all our problems; sophisticated but low-tech approaches like those of Bunker Roy and Barefoot College offer powerful solutions to some of the most pressing market failures. But one key question will be whether, in the spirit of the open source approach to software, social entrepreneurs can democratize the development, deployment, and use of the new tools needed to build new, more equitable, and more sustainable forms of wealth creation.

Gandhi was no slave to technology—indeed, he was far from it—but he would have appreciated the work of people like Ashok Khosla at Development Alternatives, based in Delhi, India. A Harvard doctorate in experimental physics seems an unlikely qualification for brick making, but when Khosla abandoned a promising scientific career to focus on issues of environment and development, he embarked on a mission to carry forward a key Gandhian concept: the democratization of knowledge. In the process, he has made massive contributions to the ability of ordinary Indians—and people of many other nationalities—to make the basic building blocks of civilized life.

In this chapter we briefly study four clusters of entrepreneurs whose ventures focus on the trends that will improve the future for a growing proportion of the burgeoning human population. In order of the sophistication of the underlying technologies, we group the technologies as follows:

- Basic building blocks, such as bricks, tiles, and water pumps

- Vehicles, particularly motorcycles and aircraft (or "wheels and wings")

- Old and new media and the associated technologies

- Twenty-first-century tools of genetics and biotechnology

For each cluster we'll describe the remarkable work of one or more of our unreasonable entrepreneurs—and explore some of the lessons they have learned in the process.

Basic Building Blocks

So great is the pace of evolution in this field, that it can be difficult to pick a representative sample—but in what follows we spotlight nine enterprises that illustrate some of the basic characteristics of how these entrepreneurs operate.

Ashok Khosla and Development Alternatives

Let's begin with Ashok Khosla, who, like so many other social and environmental entrepreneurs, has made a difference in the diverse worlds of government, education, business, and the citizen sector. After helping design and teach Harvard's first course on the environment, he set up and directed the environmental policy unit for the Indian government and later worked for the United Nations Environment Programme in Kenya. In 1983, he established the hybrid nonprofit and its spin-off social businesses with which his name is now most closely associated: Development Alternatives. Over the years, this extraordinary organization has turned out one new technology or method after another, simultaneously creating income for the poor and protecting or regenerating the environment.

Among Development Alternatives' most notable successes have been machines that produce standardized and affordable products for rural markets, such as roofing systems, compressed earthen blocks, fired bricks, recycled paper, handloom textiles, cooking stoves, briquetting presses, and biomass-based electricity. To take just one example, the TARA micro concrete roof tile kit consists of a simple machine and related tools, providing employment for five people and affordable roof tiles for thousands. The environmental benefits? The TARA vertical shaft brick kiln cuts energy use by 55 percent and emissions by 50 percent, offering an officially approved replacement for traditional technologies now banned on environmental grounds.

Development Alternatives' paper production units, meanwhile, employ forty workers to produce textured high-quality paper from rags and recycled paper. DESI Power, its electric utility, installs mini power stations in villages, fueled by weeds and agricultural waste. TARAhaat brings information technology to villages through its Internet portal, and its rapidly growing network of franchised local telecenters provides a range of information services—including educational courses, e-governance services, and Internet connec-tivity—to local people on a commercial basis.

All that is just the tip of the iceberg. The organization's fuel-efficient, low-emission stoves are now widely used in Indian homes. Local groups and official agencies use Development Alternatives' portable pollution-monitoring kits to test water and air quality in cities and towns across the country. Development Alternatives has also built more than 130 check dams to revive the water cycle of many microwatersheds. Khosla and his team estimate that, in total, the group has created more than half a million sustainable liveli-hoods across India.

The Development Alternatives story underscores how critical it is to fully understand the socioeconomic and environmental con-text in which the poor live. Khosla's appreciation of that context allowed him to design and produce a spectrum of technologies that are useful, are affordable, and improve the lives of his clients. But what happens when others—including companies and public and nongovernmental organizations—drawn by the success of such in-novations, try to replicate them in other contexts? Unfortunately, such efforts will likely fall short of producing the intended impact. In fact, one of the most common complaints heard in government and development agencies is the lack of transferability and scalabil-ity of innovative approaches spawned by social entrepreneurs work-ing at the grassroots level.

We believe the fault lies less in the innovations and their lack of transferability and more in the cut-and-paste approach that inter-mediaries bring to such undertakings. Such agencies are ill equipped to spearhead local and global replication of grassroots innovation and development. Why? Because successful social innovators like Khosla (and Fisher and Moon from KickStart, profiled next), as well as many others, have spent decades designing, implementing, and refining demand-driven approaches to complex social and en-vironmental problems. Their achievements have followed a con-tinued process of trial and error. They know the stakeholders to involve, the signals to watch for, and the pitfalls to avoid. Fortu-nately, development organizations and governments are recognizing their limitations in this sphere, drawing on the accumulated knowledge of the Khoslas of this world. And the key factor behind Khoslas's undeniable impact as a change maker, to use his own term, has been his laserlike focus on the social and environmental dimensions of value creation.

Nick Moon, Martin Fisher, and KickStart

Similar principles apply to the work of KickStart in East Africa, already mentioned in terms of its extraordinary impact on the economies of countries like Kenya (chapter 3). *Time* magazine named cofounders Nick Moon and Martin Fisher two of its *Time* Heroes in 2003.[1] Moon and Fisher had chosen a hybrid nonprofit model to identify profitable small-scale industries that can support thousands of local entrepreneurs and enable them to repay small capital investments in three to six months from start-up. KickStart also designs and markets appropriate technologies to help establish these new small businesses.

KickStart's products must meet strict criteria: among other things, they must be affordable, manually operated, energy efficient, easy to transport by bicycle or bus, and durable. As if that were not enough of a challenge, they should require minimum training to install and use and be very easy to maintain and repair. The organization designs tools for mass production and trains local manufacturers in large-scale production techniques. It then buys the products from the manufacturers and markets them to poor entrepreneurs.

KickStart's MoneyMaker foot-operated micro irrigation pumps have been identified as one of "ten inventions that will change the world" by *Newsweek* magazine.[2] So what does this mean in practice? To relate just one example, Samuel Ndungu Mburu, one of the poorest farmers in his valley in central Kenya, owned one acre of land and made only $100 a year from selling his meager crop. In desperation, he went to Nairobi to try to support his seven children. He tried selling roasted maize on the roadside but was constantly harassed by the local authorities and made too little to send home. Frustrated, he returned to his village, where he saw a Kick-Start MoneyMaker pump being sold at a local shop. He convinced the shop owner to take a down payment and let him pay the balance after his first harvest. He started growing high-value tomatoes and green beans and today rents and irrigates five acres of land, making over $1,600 profit per year. His oldest son, who has graduated from technical college, credits the MoneyMaker pump with changing his family's life. Not only was Mburu able to pay this son's college tuition and buy him a bike to get to class; but another son is now studying to be an electrician, and all the other children are in primary or secondary school.

Are Fisher and Moon concerned about others imitating their products? Quite the contrary, they insist. KickStart's goal is to subsidize the development and establishment of new technologies until they become so firmly rooted in society that many other companies step up to compete. According to Fisher, "To date, over fifty-two thousand families in Africa have escaped poverty by using our irrigation pumps and other technologies, but we have only scratched the surface. We are now working to scale our program to help many millions more."[3] Fisher and Moon are the first to acknowledge that success in meeting their wider goals will also depend on others' replicating their endeavors.

Wheels and Wings

Even well-planned development efforts often stumble because organizations tend to overlook distribution, a crucial component. For example, bricks and foot-operated pumps generally don't need to travel a great distance, but essential pharmaceuticals often come from far away. Food supplies, new drugs, vaccines, and other critical health products—including mosquito nets and condoms—are useless unless they reach their intended destination. So how can entrepreneurs get such items where they are most needed—that is, where market failures are the greatest?

That's where two exemplary organizations—Riders for Health and Air Serv International—enter the picture.

Andrea and Barry Coleman and Riders for Health

If you want to drive change, it often makes sense to use—and adapt—the tools you know best. One stunning example is provided by Andrea and Barry Coleman of Riders for Health. After a life-changing experience in Africa, the Colemans woke up to the fact that while it takes only a few hours to reach any capital in the world by plane, it can take days and many hardships to reach developing countries' more rural areas. Because the Colemans met through their common passion for motorcycle racing, the tools that were most readily in their hands were motorcycles.

The epiphany came when Andrea, herself a racer, and Barry, a journalist, accompanied motorcycle champion Randy Mamola on a trip to Somalia to visit a project he was sponsoring, an immunization day for children. They never reached the site—and the immunization day didn't happen—because their cars broke down. Thus, they came face-to-face with an ever-present barrier to effective delivery of goods and services in rural Africa, where the majority of the continent's population lives: a lack of know-how about vehicle maintenance and repair. The result, all too often, is that next-to-new motorcycles and four-wheel-drive vehicles sit in parking lots or at roadsides, left to rust and fall apart. It's a waste of money and other resources. Worse, such problems seriously hamper progress in Africa by limiting the delivery of vital health services, including the drugs and diagnostics essential for disease prevention and eradication.

So, as a first step, the Colemans became active in fund-raising for Save the Children and started a vehicle management program for the NGO in the country of Lesotho. Then, in 1996, they decided to launch Riders for Health. The organization has shown that appropriate modern technology can perform without breakdowns even across the unforgiving terrain of rural Africa. Eventually, Riders managed to halve the cost of motorcycle transportation. Today, the organization estimates that with nine hundred bikes in operation, it reaches an astonishing 11 million people with regular, reliable health care.

By using the bikes, governmental and NGO workers involved with health-related aid and other kinds of help have increased their number of visits to remote communities by at least 300 percent. In one district in Zimbabwe, malaria death rates fell by 20 percent after health workers were equipped with motorcycles. The Colemans think that leaders in the public and private sectors can learn from their success. Their advice is this: "Understand how important the 'greasy hands' part of development is. Bikes, cars, and trucks are tools, not toys. When the rubber hits the road, they can be as vital as policy, microbiology, and microfinance."[4]

As major companies become more involved in BOP markets, mainstream businesspeople become more interested in understanding what they can learn from Riders' work—and, in several cases, how they can use aspects of Riders' logistical network for their own ends. However Riders may help their business counterparts, they are pioneering some of the most important economic pathways of the new century.

Air Serv International

If there is one guarantee in the twenty-first century—alongside nagging systemic dysfunctions—it is natural or man-made disasters. An enterprise that illustrates the potential social value creation opportunities in disaster relief is Air Serv International. As some media outlets discovered during the tsunami crisis of 2004, Air Serv uses the latest technology—not motorcycles in this case, but aircraft (like the DeHavilland Dash 8, Turbine DC-3, and Antonov 32) and a wide range of helicopters. Founded in 1984 by a handful of pilots responding to the same famines that helped ignite Bob Geldof's passion to tackle hunger and poverty, Air Serv has since provided over a hundred fifty thousand mercy flights for hundreds of relief and development agencies around the world.

Working for (and largely funded by) UN agencies, the U.S. Agency for International Development, and international and local humanitarian organizations, Air Serv collaborates closely with those agencies—in effect, serving the servers.

Using single- and twin-engine aircraft in dangerous, remote, or transportation-deficient areas and larger aircraft operations to airlift food and seed, Air Serv is resolutely nonprofit—although it's not hard to imagine how profits could be made from some communities in distress. In some ways, the organization sits between models 1 and 2 in our typology. In the face of famine and flood, earthquake and war, the world's leading relief and development agencies count on (and help fund) Air Serv's unique capabilities to get their human and material cargo to those who need it. Yet the very conditions that create emergency situations often make flying a perilous task. Many of the Air Serv pilots and crew work for corporations or for airline companies but are willing to use their skills to serve the poorest of the poor, providing air transportation in some of the most dangerous and desperate situations, often at great personal risk. Indeed, sometimes fighting subsides only temporarily while an Air Serv plane swoops in to make an emergency delivery or evacuation. Often, runways are makeshift at best, navigation aids unreliable, weather conditions terrible, and alternative airports nonexistent.

"We fly where other air carriers cannot—or will not—fly," declares the Air Serv motto, "making us in a very real way the only air carrier that can get relief workers from the world's most respected humanitarian organizations where they need to go."[5] One key characteristic, as with organizations like the Red Cross and Médecins Sans Frontières, is Air Serv's absolute commitment to political neutrality. Its pilots and other volunteers are careful to remain nonpartisan: though many opposed the Iraq war, for example, they headed to Iraq to help soon after the conflict began.

"Our staunch adherence to remaining neutral in the face of conflict means we can fly to places where others may be restricted," Air Serv explains on its Web site.[6] "We are not affiliated with any government, church-based mission, corporation or other entity. As part of the first step of an emergency response, our passengers include relief assessors and doctors, nurses, water engineers and nutritionists from our fellow humanitarian organizations, including Save the Children, CARE, World Vision, Médecins Sans Frontières and many others, who must respond quickly to emergencies." Moreover, "it is often said by our fellow humanitarian workers that they fly Air Serv or they don't fly at all."

Old and New Media

Everyday miracles like motorcycles and planes tend to be taken for granted in developed markets, but not in other parts of the world. In the same way, the media that inform and entertain us every day can seem almost otherworldly to those with no access to books, radios, computers, or tools like the video cameras that activists use to record—and, in some cases, redress—environmental and human rights abuses. Let's look at what a number of entrepreneurs are doing in each of these areas.

John Wood and Room to Read

First, we'll consider books. We have already covered First Book, which focuses on getting books to young Americans, so let's begin here with a leveraged nonprofit organization (model 1) that does the same for youngsters in the developing world: Room to Read. The enterprise was founded on the beliefs that "World Change Starts with Educated Children" and that education is the key to breaking the cycle of poverty. The story began in 1998, when founder and CEO John Wood was "an overworked Microsoft executive looking for the quiet solitude of a trekking vacation."[7] While he was backpacking in the Himalayas, Wood came across a middle-aged Nepalese man who invited him to visit a nearby village school. Jumping at the chance to see the real Nepal, rather than sticking to his tourist's trek, Wood agreed—and the encounter changed his life.

The Nepalese man turned out to be an education resource officer. Wood duly discovered that despite the man's best efforts—which involved crossing high mountain passes on foot to visit schools— he had few resources to offer the schools for which he was responsible. Wood, in short, came face-to-face with a harsh reality facing millions of Nepalese children: there were almost no books. He was shocked to discover that the few books the local school had—"a Danielle Steele romance, the *Lonely Planet Guide to Mongolia*, and a few other backpacker castoffs"—were deemed so precious that they were locked up to protect them from the children.

As Wood left the village, the headmaster made a simple request: "Perhaps, Sir, you will some day come back with books."[8] When he got home, Wood e-mailed friends to ask for help in collecting children's books and says he was overwhelmed with the response: "Over three thousand books arrived within two months." The following year, he returned to Nepal, rented a team of six donkeys, and visited the village to deliver the books.

On that trip, he also made a decision to leave the corporate world, which he did in late 1999, to start Room to Read. His goal? To marry the business practices he had learned at Microsoft with his new mission to provide the lifelong gift of education to millions of children in the developing world. In his memoir, *Leaving Microsoft to Change the World*, he explains, "Did it really matter how many copies of Windows we sold in Taiwan this month when there were millions of children without access to books?"[9] With 750 million illiterate adults worldwide and 100 million children without access to school, he set out to build a nonprofit venture "with the scalability of Starbucks and the compassion of Mother Teresa."[10]

Ask Wood about his biggest single challenge to date, and he responds:

There is no road map for what we are doing, so we've had to make a lot of it up as we went along. For example, there are virtually no children's books in languages like Nepali and Khmer and Lao because the parents are too poor to afford them, so the publishers have no business case to publish. It's a problem almost as old as the Himalayas, and until we get it right, millions of children will remain illiterate. So we've taken an entrepreneurial approach by recruiting and training local authors and artists. We now have dozens of local versions of Dr. Seuss working with us to create brightly colored and culturally relevant children's books—over 150 to date, with an additional 100 being produced per year, in eleven languages.[11]

Follow up with a question about what government and business leaders need to learn from the Room to Read experience, and he replies, "The state of today's world demands that we help the citizen sector to scale at the same pace that blue-chip companies grow when they see market opportunities. It won't do any good to throw billions of dollars at global poverty unless there is an efficient and *scalable* citizen sector that can deploy those funds. Until that happens, we will never make poverty history."[12]

What the Room to Read story tells us, in part, is that one of the great assets in the new century is going to be the people with business experience who retire—and then find that they want to stay active, to get engaged, to create some sort of enduring legacy. Whereas early entrants no doubt felt like mutants, the success of the approaches pioneered by John Wood and others will assure future generations of entrepreneurs that they can make a real difference—so long as they think about (and build in) scalability from the outset.

Rory Stear and Freeplay Energy

Perhaps even more powerful than books is radio, the most widely used medium for mass communication in developing countries. In this space one of the most influential social entrepreneurs has been Rory Stear of Freeplay Energy. Stear, a serial entrepreneur, came across the original windup radio after his then business partner saw it on a BBC program. Stear secured the worldwide rights to the technology, developed it further to make it commercially viable, and adapted it for practical use under arduous rural conditions. He then set up Freeplay Energy in 1994 as a commercial, model 3 company. Among early investors were Anita and Gordon Roddick of the Body Shop International.

Since then, the company has developed patented windup technology, coupled with solar energy, for radios, flashlights, water purifiers, mobile phone chargers, medical instruments, and standalone power generators. In the process, Freeplay has increased the potential impact of ventures that focus on public health, education, and income generation for poor and rural communities, thereby helping eradicate poverty and improve quality of life.

Freeplay radios do not require grid-supply electricity or batteries: a few minutes of winding or some solar energy provide hours of listening. Since the company released its first product in 1996, more than four hundred thousand of its self-powered radios have been sent to sub-Saharan Africa and other parts of the developing world, providing continuous access to information to more than 8 million people.

As of 2007, Freeplay had sold more than 5 million products worldwide. The largest markets by far are North America and Europe—particularly in the wake of the 9/11 attacks, when many Americans stocked up their emergency bunkers. Outdoor enthusiasts, environmentalists, emergency preparedness workers, and emergency response workers are also avid purchasers of Freeplay products.

The company has channeled the benefits of these high-volume sales in affluent markets to support product development for the less fortunate. In 1998, Stear established the Freeplay Foundation as part of this social agenda and brought Kristine Pearson on board as its founding executive director in early 1999. The foundation funded the development of the Lifeline radio, designed specifically for humanitarian and development use, and subsidizes the Lifeline's purchase price for such markets. The Freeplay Foundation's work is focused in Africa, where the high cost of batteries and low levels of electricity keep the poor from using radios to access basic information. Each Lifeline radio reaches a listening group of at least twenty people. The foundation also develops local partnerships with radio stations to help ensure that they broadcast appropriate content.

When asked to name the biggest challenge Freeplay has faced to date, Stear replies, "The whole Freeplay Energy project has been an extremely ambitious undertaking. Not only were we developing new technology from scratch, but we also were designing and implementing a highly unconventional hybrid business model, which included a separate, not-for-profit entity: the foundation. Balancing the realities of running a new, fast-growing commercial enterprise with supporting a hybrid not-for-profit contained a myriad of tensions, which needed to be carefully managed."[13] His greatest challenge for the next few years? "Now that both entities—the company and the autonomous Freeplay Foundation—are well established, the greatest challenge is turning the company into a broader-based, off-the-grid energy supplier and addressing both the opportunity and the obligation of providing access to power to the 35 percent of the world's population that have none and the . . . 35 percent who have limited access."

Finally, what makes Freeplay Energy and its foundation different from ordinary profit-making companies with their own charitable arms? "Freeplay has never seen the foundation as a charitable arm," Stear says, "but rather as a stand-alone entity designed to address access-to-energy issues where the company can never go, which is basically providing access to energy to the 'last billion' people. We work in partnership with them—it is not a master-servant relationship between a donor and recipient."

One key message here is that mainstream companies seeking to achieve leverage in their social and environmental programs have a range of entrepreneurial partners to choose from. The flip side, however, is that this is not like walking down a supermarket aisle and picking products off the shelf: these entrepreneurs have a very clear idea of the sort of corporate partners they want to work with, and they are prepared to invest the necessary effort to ensure a good strategic fit.

Gillian Caldwell and Witness

The step beyond radio is video in the service of human rights. While Freeplay Energy is a commercially viable, publicly traded enterprise, it is hard to imagine setting up a for-profit human rights campaigning organization. So, as executive director of Witness, a hybrid nonprofit organization based in New York, Gillian Caldwell spent her days helping others film shocking examples of human rights abuse.[14] Involved in social justice work her entire life, she first recognized the value of powerful imagery as a young girl when she saw a painting by Leon Golub in her mother's art gallery. "The picture showed a CIA-trained mercenary urinating on a political prisoner, bound and tied and lying on the floor," she recalls. "His torturer stood over him, urinating, his back to the viewer. An accomplice turned his head around so that his gaze caught the viewer straight in the eye. Golub made everyone who looked at his paintings a 'witness' in the same way—and left them wondering what they were going to do in response."[15]

Later, while working as an attorney with the civil rights movement, Caldwell took part in an undercover investigation of the Russian mafia's involvement in trafficking women from the former Soviet Union into forced prostitution. From 1995 to 1998, as codirector of the Global Survival Network, she worked with Steve Galster as he posed as a buyer for a dummy company interested in importing women into the United States. Caldwell and Galster used hidden cameras to film transactions with the Russian mafia and eventually incorporated those images into the documentary *Bought & Sold*. Footage from the film was the subject of television programs on ABC News, the BBC, and CNN, and inspired a major story in the *New York Times*. This evidence helped convince President Clinton to issue an executive order allocating $10 million to fight violence against women, with an emphasis on trafficking, and also contributed to the UN's passage of a transnational protocol designed to prevent trafficking. The U.S. Congress passed the Trafficking Victims Protections Act in 2000.

The success of *Bought & Sold* prompted Witness to hire Caldwell as its executive director in 1998. The organization had been founded in 1992 by musician and activist Peter Gabriel, who took one of the early consumer handheld video cameras on a global tour with Amnesty International. Inspired by the activists he met, Gabriel came up with the idea of putting video cameras in their hands so they could capture evidence of abuses that governments could not cover up. Four years later, in the wake of the Rodney King beating by the Los Angeles police, Gabriel raised seed funding for Witness from the Reebok Human Rights Foundation, and the Lawyers Committee for Human Rights (now known as Human Rights First) agreed to house the program.

When Caldwell came on board as executive director, she realized that supplying cameras to activists was not enough. "I knew we couldn't just drop off a camera and walk away," she explains. "We had to help with every phase of the process, with training, distribution and the advocacy phase of each project." Under her leadership, Witness began providing in-depth technical and tactical training to human rights groups and has partnered with groups in more than sixty countries. "The point is not just, 'What's the problem?' but also 'What's the solution?'" Caldwell explains.[16]

Ask her what her biggest challenge is going to be in the coming years, and she replies, "Staying evolutionary so that we can take advantage of rapid innovations of technology." What can leaders in business and government learn from her work? "The most powerful and lasting solutions to the problems we face exist at a local level," she insists. "Each and every one of us has the power to change the world, if we believe we can and have the right tools at our disposal."[17]

The human rights agenda is evolving rapidly around the world. The combination of energetic campaigners like Gillian Caldwell and the latest digital imaging, recording, and communication technologies means that governments and businesses alike will be taken to task when they are directly or indirectly complicit in abuses. A key question for business leaders, therefore, will be whether to wait for such issues to erupt out of the blue—or to dive in, engage, learn, and help change things for the better. There may still be mishaps along the way, but in the end, sustainable markets are only built when people's human and civil rights are respected as a matter of course.

Richard Jefferson and Cambia

We conclude this brief survey of efforts to democratize technology by looking at a field that would have seemed wildly futuristic to Gandhi: biological innovation. To simplify the task, let's look over the shoulder of molecular biologist Richard Jefferson. A serial entrepreneur, Jefferson is on a crusade to free the tools of science from wildly broad patent rights held in obscure ways by a wide range of players whose primary interest is profit.

For thousands of years, Jefferson notes, biological innovation in agriculture was cooperative. By sharing the trial-and-error processes, farmers improved crop varieties and livestock. But the explosion in the power of science to improve agriculture, medicine, health, and environment in the past thirty years has been accompanied by a rush to lay claim to this knowledge by public- and private-sector scientists who have patented their developments, privatizing the tools that previously had been shared by all. As a result, the food and health industries have come to be dominated by large multinationals that target high-margin products and big markets. Consequently, advances in biotechnology are not being applied to poverty or hunger alleviation or eradication of neglected diseases that affect the poor, because the small profit margins and markets preclude the development of key innovations in these areas by small and medium-size enterprises.

As Jefferson explains:

Consider the wheel, perhaps a six-spoked wheel. In some ways, it is the most fundamental tool in society. It has countless uses unanticipated by its inventors; most were made by people who are not wheel-builders. The wheel is only useful when it does something, such as moving a cart; its economic value to society lies not in the price of the wheel, but in the wealth created through the use of the wheel. If it takes all six spokes for this wheel to turn, and each of these spokes is potentially different in some way, we have a good metaphor for a modern biological technology. Increasingly, biological technologies are not self-contained; rather they are interdependent technologies that require multiple key methods and components to function. If one spoke is withheld, no wheel is built. If one spoke is broken, the wheel will jam. And then the cart cannot move forward. By analogy, the most powerful technologies can be considered as "wheels," requiring a number of "spokes" to function. For instance, the ability to transfer a gene to a crop plant may require dozens of individually patented, discrete technologies. Denial of access to any one of these "spokes" obstructs not only the use of the technology, but its improvement. Only when the core technology is in place, with full functionality, can it be subject to iterative and cooperative shaping to meet diverse users' needs.[18]

To unlock the stranglehold on the tools of science and democratize advances in biotechnology, Jefferson founded Cambia, a hybrid, nonprofit, international research institute in Canberra, Australia. Cambia has become a global leader in the open source movement for the life sciences, providing practical services and tools including the Patent Lens information service to help innovators navigate through the huge, often confusing labyrinth of existing patents. Patent Lens collates and harmonizes data from several national and international patent offices. Cambia has created technological license platforms and templates, similar to open source licenses, through its Biological Open Source (BiOS) Initiative. Under these legally binding agreements, the new technology is available—royalty-free for further research or to create new products—to any party agreeing to freely share any improvements to the technology with other license holders, even if the improvement has been patented. This creates a dynamic, investment-secure environment for innovation on these platforms. And Jefferson is positioning his efforts to drive a broader approach toward open innovation in all realms of the life sciences.[19]

Multinational corporations (MNCs) claim it is the costs of researching and developing agricultural and medical products that drive their need to protect intellectual property. Yet, as Jefferson maintains, the open source approach to developing biotechnology allows for many to share the costs, dramatically changing the demographics of problem solving.[20]

Jefferson is not against intellectual property rights guaranteed by copyright, patents, and other legislation. In fact, he holds the patents on a DNA-based molecular tool—the GUS reporter—that is one of the most widely used tools in biotechnology. The concerns he and other open source advocates have are about what kinds of scientific outcomes qualify for protection and how the exercise of intellectual property rights ends up blocking the access of other scientists and entrepreneurs to the tools needed for innovation. Jefferson feels that the norm this establishes alienates and excludes many creative problem solvers from using science as part of social enterprise.

The open source science movement has already attracted a diverse range of supporters, including governments, multinational corporations, large philanthropic organizations, and research and local science institutions. But as one can imagine, there may be others who view open source science with alarm. What happens if all these approaches create unexpected problems, such as new weed species or highly infectious agents? What happens if al-Qaeda or a similar organization adopts and adapts these technologies? Jefferson's response is that the transparency and accountability afforded by open source approaches provide better protection against abuses than the more stealthy approaches favored by many companies and governments in particular.

What lessons can we draw from the cases in this chapter? First, social and environmental entrepreneurs need to build legitimacy for their ideas and approaches: it can take an enormous amount of energy to persuade others that what social entrepreneurs propose will transform ineffective and unjust systems and practices. Second, and closely related to the first, these entrepreneurs must find ways to gain access to political, corporate, and thought leaders who will embrace innovative approaches and then leverage those connections to drive wider implementation. And, third, such entrepreneurs also must work out how to attract sufficient—and sufficiently patient—capital to develop, test, refine, deploy, and scale their initiatives.

But, perhaps most fundamentally of all, if they are to achieve anything like their full potential, these entrepreneurs must work out how to change the system—a theme to which we now turn.

SIX

Changing the System

I F THE ENTREPRENEURS profiled in previous chapters could agree on anything, it would be that the current system is dysfunctional. Some parts do work (to the advantage of privileged communities and classes), but overall, the twentieth-century governance, market, and social systems we have inherited are ill suited for the twenty-first century. So it should come as no surprise to find that one key characteristic of many leading social and, to a degree, environmental entrepreneurs is that they seek to change the system, tackling social, environmental, and governance challenges at the source.

To take a sports analogy, some people may choose to change the disposition of players on the pitch or to redesign the playing field, but a few rare individuals work to change the rules of the game—or even the game itself.

There's a bit of the game changer in most entrepreneurs; many seek to influence government policy, market rules, the educational system, or whatever else they think it will take to reach their objectives. But while some seek to change the rules of the game, others think to do so only when and where those rules bump up against the wider reality in uncomfortable ways.

Historically, many game changers have come from the worlds of science and technology. Samuel Plimsoll was one, with his extraordinary decades-long effort to force the shipping industry to adopt what eventually became known as the "Plimsoll line." Thomas Edison was one, too, when he helped switch on the world to electricity, as were Henry Ford with his mass production line, James Watson and Francis Crick with their cracking of the basic human genetic code, and Tim Berners-Lee with his original operating code for the World Wide Web and his ongoing work on the Semantic Web.

In addition to science and technology, today's social entrepreneurs are exploring new approaches to governance, property rights, and market transformations. For example, people like Peruvian economist Hernando de Soto work hard to promote the kind of governance and market systems that will ensure better living conditions for populations in developing countries.[1] In China, de Soto notes, "only 250 million out of 1.3 billion Chinese have property rights and the right to hold assets in the private sector."[2] Once again, someone needs to change the system before the forces of entrepreneurship can be fully unleashed.

Other entrepreneurs, too, know that there are great advantages in shaping larger systems to support their purpose. A striking example is Gary Cohen of Health Care Without Harm, an international coalition of hospitals and health care systems, medical and nursing professionals, and related stakeholder groups. Its ambitious aim? "To transform the health care industry worldwide, without compromising patient safety or care, so that it is ecologically sustainable, and no longer a source of harm to public health or the environment."[3] Health Care Without Harm exists, in part, to phase out a wide range of toxic chemicals and materials that can impact the health of patients, medical staff, the public, and the environment.

To get a better sense of how—and where—social and environmental entrepreneurs are trying to change the system, we examine six areas where real progress is being made:

- Transparency

- Accountability

- Certification

- Land reform

- Emission trading

- Value and valuation

Again, for each area we spotlight real people and organizations that are expending considerable energy and other resources to make a difference. Mainstream companies that get involved in such initiatives early not only have an opportunity to shape future market rules but also get the jump on their competitors. The stragglers may find themselves struggling to catch up with some of the most important endeavors and opportunity spaces of the twenty-first century.

Transparency

Reasonable people make do with the information they can track down. They accept that information is always imperfect, and they make the best of things. Unreasonable people, on the other hand, believe that transparency is a necessary condition for political change, which, in turn, is a necessary condition for sustained, equitable progress. One man has stood head and shoulders above the rest in turning the world into a goldfish bowl, affording much higher levels of transparency and accountability. He is Peter Eigen, who cofounded Transparency International (TI), an organization dedicated to the battle against bribery and corruption.[4]

Transparency does not guarantee system change, but it is often a critical first step. Eigen, originally a World Bank official with vast experience in Africa and Latin America, had argued unsuccessfully that the World Bank should address these problems in its programs. Many of his colleagues at the Bank thought him unreasonable in pushing for a state of affairs that offended so many vested interests.

But Eigen and his unreasonably determined colleagues made it clear that they were serious. After considerable discussion, the founding group decided that their initial objective—launching a publication to draw attention to corrupt actions by specific businesses—was unlikely to have the desired impact. Instead of going head-on at governments and business, they concluded that coalition building was the real key to success. Instead of criticizing from a distance, TI would join in the search for solutions. Today, this tiny group has turned into a global force, with national chapters around the world.

The founders shared the experience of seeing firsthand the devastating effects of corruption—particularly corruption across borders. They argued that in many parts of the world, the system was deeply diseased. And they knew that if you want to change the system, you must have—or must develop—convening power. Officially launched in 1993, TI soon leveraged its large list of contacts to organize its first conference, bringing together such figures as Oscar Arias Sánchez, the Nobel Peace Prize laureate and former president of Costa Rica; Ahmedou Ould-Abdallah, the former foreign minister of Mauritania; Ronald MacLean-Abaroa, the former foreign minister of Bolivia; and Olusegun Obasanjo, then of the African Leadership Forum and later president of Nigeria. One early target was the regulatory frameworks in most countries that allowed people to offer and give bribes abroad.[5] In some countries bribes were formally tax deductible.

But TI isn't just another gathering of the world's political elite. One key to the organization's success has been its nurturing of an unusual coalition of actors from civil society, business, and government. Although it does not expose individual cases, viewing that as the work of journalists, TI does see access to information as a key weapon in the battle against corruption. Its approach of publishing an annual country-by-country listing of whose hands are dirty—and whose are clean—has been hugely successful. The Corruption Perceptions Index (CPI) provides a snapshot of the views of decision makers and businesspeople, both locals and expatriates, about the level of corruption in a given country. That, the TI

Web site argues, "is an incredibly important indicator of the image a country conveys to investors and potential business partners. A poor score in the CPI is a clear signal that a government has to make drastic changes—and to be seen to be doing so."[6]

This is only the start, however. At best, TI acts as a gadfly, goading government and business leaders to act. Its campaigns encourage media awareness and coverage of such issues, but effective government policy making, regulation, and enforcement are needed to develop sustainable traction in the war against corruption. As globalization continues, these efforts will need to expand around the world, which will entail the fundamental rewiring of existing institutions or the creation of new ones.

Accountability

Reasonable people know that they can expect a limited degree of accountability from leaders in the public and private sectors. They understand that power implies privilege and, with it, a human tendency to skirt the rules or reach for more than one's share, ignoring the consequences for others. Unreasonable people, on the other hand, set out to change the order of things. They insist on developing new mechanisms of accountability for effective, equitable, and sustainable social change. Recent years have seen a proliferation of such initiatives, several of which use approaches similar to that of Transparency International. Why? Because transparency and accountability generally go hand in hand.

Countries are competitive—and companies even more so. Therefore, if you were to devise a credible methodology and produce a set of national or corporate rankings on just about any subject, you would likely attract attention from those being ranked. SustainAbility and the United Nations Environment Programme did just that in 1994, when they began benchmarking and ranking companies in a series of studies, variously labeled over time as environmental, social, sustainability, nonfinancial, and extrafinancial reports. The two organizations more recently partnered with the risk-rating agency Standard & Poor's, and the program—and its influence—have continued to grow.[7]

On a larger scale is the Global Reporting Initiative (GRI), which encourages companies to report on their triple-bottom-line performance—that is, the extent to which they are reducing their negative economic, social, and environmental footprints and building new kinds of blended value. The GRI was the brainchild of Bob Massie, who at the time headed the Coalition for Environmentally Responsible Economies (Ceres), a U.S.-based coalition of investors and environmentalists.[8]

Ceres's goal for the GRI is to leverage the power of institutional investors in holding corporations accountable for environmental sustainability in all those corporations' activities.[9] Massie, trained as a historian and a theologian with a doctorate from Harvard Business School, brings a unique perspective to the issues of transparency and accountability. "As a historian, one learns to look at the world not through the perspective of a few years or decades, but through trends that last over centuries," he told participants in the 2006 launch of the GRI's G3 reporting guidelines.[10] Together with the associated protocols and sector supplements, the guidelines are designed to help any business or other organization to produce consistent, useful sustainability reports. But Massie sees all of this in a much wider context: "And as a theologian, in my case a Christian theologian, one is encouraged to think about questions at an even greater scale. And one becomes comfortable thinking about the question of meaning. The creation of meaning, the understanding of why we do things always takes place in community."

Massie noted that when the GRI was launched, "many people assumed that its mission was too bold, its resources [were] too few, and the historical differences and resentments between the parties whose cooperation would be required [were] too great. By any objective measurement, their analysis seemed to be correct. But fortunately there were enough people who decided that despite the probability of failure, they wanted to participate in the experiment."

Massie went on to say:

We all knew that a corporation, just like a government, or a school, was an organism that pulled in resources, transformed them, and emitted products, knowledge, and waste, and that only some of the inputs and outputs were captured by the form of measurement we refer to as accounting. As a result, our idea of what it is to create wealth—real, lasting wealth [and] genuine, enduring capital—is hopelessly primitive and unsophisticated. And we believed that the purpose of all of these measurements was not to please any one group—investors, or consumers, or managers, or stakeholders—but to help to make progress toward the more elusive question of purpose, of trajectory, what the Greeks called the *telos*.

In conclusion, he remarked:

The question "What is the purpose of the firm?" is a subset of a larger question: "[W]hat is the goal of our human community?" The more we understand what a firm does and does not do, can and cannot do, the more we as managers, board members, investors, consumers, government leaders can ask ourselves whether this is indeed what we want it to do, whether we are expecting too little or too much. The GRI was built on the notion that transparency would allow everyone to see—and thus to begin to accept intellectually and morally—their own responsibility for the choices that we face today and [in] the future. In that too we have begun to succeed.

These are deep questions for most corporate boards, but a growing number of key actors are placing them on the business agenda. They include Alice Tepper Marlin of Social Accountability International, with its SA8000 social auditing standard, and Simon Zadek of AccountAbility, with its AA1000 standard for organizational accountability. The trend is spreading to the sensitive area of NGO accountability, too. Over a decade ago in India, for example, Bunker Roy of Barefoot College called for an NGO code of conduct. At the time, it was a groundbreaking and controversial, but visionary and much-needed, initiative.

Roy sought to standardize social auditing to render the Indian voluntary social sector more transparent, effective, reliable, and accountable. In the firestorm of controversy that followed, the social sector divided into opposing camps of pro- and antitransparency advocates. As a result, Roy's campaign failed to achieve its main goals, and to date, Barefoot College has been the only community-based organization in India that has opened its auditing books to the public. Still, the campaign did influence the more recent creation of the Credibility Alliance in India, spearheaded by followers of Roy's example.

Here again, however, voluntary efforts only take us so far. They are certainly better than nothing, but while initiatives like the GRI may attract a few thousand supporting companies, a single giant company like Wal-Mart has something like sixty-one thousand suppliers in its vast supply chain. If companies on that scale begin to embrace the benefits of new forms of transparency and accountability, the movement will advance dramatically. Nevertheless, as we will see in the conclusion of this book, national and international governments are crucial actors here, too. Why? In the end, these are political questions, and government will need to develop and enforce the rules for twenty-first century society and its markets.

Certification

Certification and other assurance processes are crucial steps toward ensuring acceptable conditions for producers and high standards for consumers and investors. Many of the accountability initiatives mentioned in the previous section, including the GRI, offer some form of certification. Other organizations certify social performance (e.g., Social Accountability International) or environmental performance (e.g., the Forest Stewardship Council, the Marine Stewardship Council, and other initiatives in such areas as organic agriculture, labor conditions, and workforce diversity). To learn how their efforts can transform a sector like coffee production or retailing, consider the work of Paul Rice, president and CEO of TransFair USA, the leading fair trade organization in the United States.[11]

When asked for TransFair's elevator pitch, Rice replies, "It all depends on what sort of audience I had in the elevator. But for the average layman, fair trade is about helping farmers become independent and self-reliant through direct, equitable market linkage, about helping farmers and their communities escape from poverty without relying on international aid."[12] What about TransFair? "That's simple: We're the only certifier of fair trade products in the USA. In the coffee area, we have signed agreements with over six hundred coffee companies, including Starbucks, Procter & Gamble, and Green Mountain Coffee Roasters, and fair-trade certified products are now in more than forty thousand U.S. retail outlets."

Fair trade has a direct effect on farmers in the developing world. "It's about the farmer getting a dramatically higher price for his or her product," Rice explains. "We're talking about fair trade companies paying $1.26 per pound of coffee, and more for a fairly traded organic product, compared with a world price of around $0.65. And when you get down to the farm level—for example, in Nicaragua, where farmers are selling to people they call 'coyotes,' the price is even lower—around $0.20. If you subtract between $0.15 and $0.25 for their costs, farmers are something like $0.80 per pound better off."

This is especially important today. Why? "In recent years, the price of coffee fell to its lowest level in fifty years," Rice replies. "The 30 million coffee farmers in Latin America, Asia, and Africa could not even put out food on the table, much less cover their production costs." Many were forced to sell their land and migrate to cities. In Colombia, farmers were replacing coffee with coca plants, fueling the global drug trade. TransFair is working to establish fair trade practices as the gold standard of sustainability for a range of agricultural products raised in developing countries and sold in the United States, including coffee, tea, cocoa, rice, sugar, fresh fruit, and cut flowers.

Rice came to fair trade by way of the mountainous Segovias region of Nicaragua, where he worked for eleven years as a rural development specialist. In the process, he became distressed by the failure of most aid projects to help people solve their own problems. So he founded the successful Prodecoop, a consortium of some fifty cooperatives representing twenty-five hundred small organic coffee farmers in northern Nicaragua, and began selling on favorable terms to fair trade buyers in Europe.

The experience convinced Rice of the transformational power of fair trade. In fact, the business even helped pull together former enemies born from the Sandinista era of the 1980s in Nicaragua, when the country was torn apart by internal conflict and when revenge killings were the order of the day. "And then the Sandinistas were voted out," he recalls, "and a huge number of programs supporting small coffee farmers were shut down. I lost my job at the department of agriculture—and, in retrospect, that was a blessing in disguise. It forced me to rethink what I was doing and take a more market-focused, entrepreneurial approach."

Subsequently, Rice served as strategy consultant and development adviser to over twenty cooperative enterprises throughout Latin America and Asia, helping them become more competitive, democratic, and self-reliant. Then, in 1994, Rice returned to the United States to enroll at the Haas School of Business at UC Berkeley, where he wrote his thesis as a business plan for what would become TransFair.

So, did the money come easily when he launched the company? "We never did raise enough money," he laughs. "In the end, the Ford Foundation's Mexican branch gave us $100,000. We had to decide whether to launch anyway—and did. We figured we had to prove the basic concept. And it was tough. Twice in the first two years, I didn't take a salary. But then, in the second year, Green Mountain and Starbucks came in, and the thing snowballed." He describes TransFair's impact on the specialty coffee industry as akin to a "paradigm shift." The basic idea is to create a new business model that makes it profitable for U.S. companies to pay higher prices and develop long-term relationships with family farmers in the global south. Whereas much of the antiglobalization movement sees free trade and markets as the enemy, TransFair helps farming communities pursue opportunities afforded by the global market.

Although he is far from 100 percent invested in the Starbucks business model, Rice stresses that, as a company, Starbucks is radically more responsible than others—such as Kraft, Procter & Gamble, and Nestlé—who, he believes, have led the industry in a "race to the bottom," often seeming to be in pursuit of the "cheapest, nastiest coffee." But Rice thinks that approach is on the way out. "People are defecting from coffee that stinks," he notes. "The specialty coffee sector has gone from 2 percent to 55 percent of the market in thirty years." Fair trade has captured 15 percent of the specialty market, and a high proportion of fairly traded products are organic (85 percent of TransFair's coffee, for example, and 100 percent of its tea and bananas are organic).

All this is part of TransFair's push to link fair trade with quality, often using tactics Rice calls "guerrilla marketing." For example, he managed to recruit actor Martin Sheen, fresh from winning a clutch of Emmys for his role in *The West Wing*, for a series of public service announcements on TV in 2002. Sheen appeared, looking presidential, cradling a cup of fair trade coffee and saying, "I choose fair trade. So should you." In the end, certification is only part of the battle: even the hottest product has to be seen as cool and be both accessible and affordable. Where these conditions are met, however, certification can reinforce the connection between those who lobby for higher standards and those who buy (or might buy) the products and services produced as a result.

Land Reform

However powerful transparency, accountability, and certification may be, there are many broader areas in which countries need to be politically and legally rewired.

In many countries, for example, land and property reform is a necessary condition for progress, as Hernando de Soto has long argued. Roy Prosterman, known as the "lawyer for the landless," has fought long and hard for that cause. That is not how he started off in life, however. A Harvard Law School graduate, he enjoyed a successful career with one of the oldest and most prestigious law firms in New York City. Over time, he became distressed by the vast sums of money corporations were spending on legal fees to defend their interests against consumers. Eventually, he left the practice and, at the invitation of the dean of the University of Washington School of Law, started teaching there. Then he came upon an article about land reform in Latin America that changed his life.

Inspired by a new life mission, Prosterman jumped in with both feet in 1966, founding the Rural Development Institute (RDI) on a shoestring. Its objective was to help reform the rural land policies of the world's poorest countries so that their farmers could gain land ownership.[13] After decades of work in land reform, Prosterman and his institute have built legal capacity in all thirty-five countries that have sought their help to date. The RDI lawyers, generally from the countries where they work, are young and committed men and women, willing to work hard at significantly less than their counterparts in mainstream law firms. Because of RDI's efforts, 70 million farmers have gained ownership rights to about 62 million acres, close to 2 percent of the world's arable land. In addition, Prosterman and his colleagues conduct intensive field research, discovering how farmers perceive their situation and needs.

Consider RDI's work in China. That giant country has to feed well over a billion people on only 9 percent of the world's arable land. To meet this challenge, it must increase crop yields, slow the loss of agricultural land to urban expansion, and bring uncultivated or environmentally degraded land into sustainable agricultural production. In service of these goals, RDI has worked hand in hand with the China Institute for Reform and Development to develop and promote the Land Management Law. This trailblazing piece of legislation provides thirty-year land-use rights for farmers, thus ensuring the long-term availability of agricultural acreage for 900 million rural citizens, 75 percent of the country's population.

In a country like China, however, enforcement can be a major issue because of widespread corruption. To help tackle this challenge, RDI has also set up regional legal-aid centers to inform farmers about their rights and help them in the exercise thereof, which advances the rule of law in the countryside. Although some may argue that the law profession has done as much to hamper as to build trust among citizens, sustainable economies of the future have to be built on sound legal foundations—and China has a long, long way to go before it is likely to suffer from the sort of legal power abuses seen in the United States.

Emission Trading

Many people dislike the idea that the rich can pay to pollute, an argument often hurled at programs that put a price on pollution to create economic incentives for investment in clean technologies. While some see emission trading as a way of letting business and other polluters off the hook, others see a system that rewards responsible behavior (because the greenest companies actually earn money by selling emission credits) and that exacts a steep price from the worst offenders. Moreover, by turning the spotlight on the relevant corporate environmental performance and wider trading patterns, these markets encourage consumers to identify and seek out more ecofriendly strategies. The potential for positive change can be enormous when the pricing is well judged, the trading mechanisms professionally handled, and the entire system policed by open, transparent, and strategically minded governments.

Thus, a handful of innovators worldwide are working to reprogram financial markets so that they take into account new forms of value creation—or destruction. These advocates for system change believe that the only way to push markets in the right direction is to revisit the pricing of key resources and assets. These people want markets, business, and products, as Ernst Ulrich von Weizsäcker once put it, to "tell the truth"—including the truth about their social and environmental footprints. Many extraordinary individuals are at work on this front, but two in particular stand out: Richard Sandor of the Chicago Climate Exchange and Tessa Tennant of the Carbon Disclosure Project.

Richard Sandor and the Chicago Climate Exchange

Walk into Richard Sandor's office in Chicago, and you pass wall after wall of stunning black-and-white photographs, a huge collection of historic images reflecting his fascination with diverse—often revolutionary—thinkers. Among them are Albert Einstein, Fidel Castro, and Man Ray. Unlike Castro, however, Sandor set out to transform the world by transforming the financial markets. He is the man behind the Chicago Climate Exchange (CCX), North America's only—and the world's first—greenhouse gas emission registry, reduction, and trading system for all six identified greenhouse gases (GHGs).[14] When President George W. Bush refused to join much of the rest of the world in signing the Kyoto Protocol to control climate change, Sandor jumped in to establish a nongovernmental alternative. "Governments don't make markets, traders do," he declared. "I'm a trader, let's make a market."[15] So on December 12, 2003, CCX started to trade carbon emission offsets. Such offsets allow individuals, organizations, and businesses to cut the impact of the carbon dioxide they emit by paying for carbon-reduction efforts elsewhere, generally where it is more economical to do so.

CCX member companies and organizations make a voluntary —but legally binding—commitment to reduce GHG emissions. By the end of phase 1 (December, 2006), all members were due to have cut their direct emissions 4 percent below their baseline emissions from 1998 to 2001. Phase 2, extending through 2010, requires all members to reduce GHG emissions 6 percent below their baseline. At the time of this writing, the exchange members included

American Electric Power, Ford, STMicroelectronics, DuPont, Motorola, and the City of Chicago. They may have joined CCX for different reasons, but all appreciated the opportunity to use the market to begin to tackle climate change.

Hunter Lovins is another environmental entrepreneur and an avid admirer of Sandor's work. Her organization, Natural Capitalism, is also a member of CCX. She says:

> It works like this: I fly around a lot. So my company bought carbon reduction credits from a company that reduced its emissions by an equal or greater amount. They make money, I pay money. My office recently signed on to get all of our electricity from wind power. Were I a big enough player to be a trader on the exchange, I could sell my reduction of coal fired power to someone else, who hasn't yet figured out how to reduce their emissions. Ultimately, this will be a very big business, not only because we have to do it, but because reducing our use of energy can be done very profitably. DuPont, a member of the exchange, has set itself a goal of reducing its emissions of GHGs by 65 percent by 2010, and by then getting 10 percent of its energy and 25 percent of its feedstocks from renewables.[16]

Lovins concludes:

> Clearly, it would be better if all emitters of GHGs were required to begin to reduce their assault on the stability of [the planet's atmosphere]. But even were the U.S. to continue its stance that solving this problem will hurt the economy, Richard Sandor has moved the game. He and his colleagues at CCX have not only set up the underlying mechanisms, and established a third party verification process, [but have also] showed their members that the process of reducing their use of energy and thus their emissions confers such very real competitive business advantages as enhancement of brand, reduction of costs, and encouragement of innovation.

Tessa Tennant and the Carbon Disclosure Project

Tessa Tennant has been another innovator in terms of systemic change. She has worked in social investment since 1987, cofounding the United Kingdom's first equity investment fund for sustainable development in 1988. She stresses the key importance of pioneers like Alice Tepper-Marlin, then of the Council on Economic Priorities (CEP), and Steven Lydenberg, of Kinder, Lydenberg, Domini & Co. (KLD), in driving the 1987 landmark book, *Rating America's Corporate Conscience*.[17] But often the key test for such pioneers is what others build on their foundations.

Tennant also underscores the importance not just of individuals, what she dubs—in deference to our title—"unreasonable teams."[18] This, she says, was key to the even more influential Carbon Disclosure Project (CDP), which she also cofounded.[19] This nonprofit group encourages large numbers of institutional investors to sign a collective global request for disclosing GHG emission information. Launched in 2000 at 10 Downing Street, official home of the U.K. prime minister, CDP has sent its petition annually to the *Financial Times* 500 companies and, in 2007, expanded its reach to over twenty four hundred companies.[20]

The CDP Web site is the world's largest registry of corporate GHG emissions. The fourth CDP survey, based on a questionnaire and completed on February 1, 2006, garnered endorsements from 211 institutional investors with assets of more than $31 trillion. Seventy-two percent (or a total of 360) of the *Financial Times* 500 companies responded, with 87 percent of those indicating that they saw climate change as presenting business risks or opportunities—or both.

Over time, ventures like CCX and CDP will encourage—and, in some cases, force—business leaders to take greater account of carbon dynamics in their business models and strategies. Meanwhile, Tennant has been tackling an even greater challenge: opening up Asia to the potential of socially responsible investment. To this end, she cofounded the Association for Sustainable & Responsible Investment in Asia (ASrIA) in 2000. ASrIA is a nonprofit association promoting corporate responsibility and sustainable investment practices in the Asia Pacific region.[21] Its members include investment institutions managing over $4 trillion in assets, although membership is open to any organization with an interest in sustainable investment.

Central to ASrIA's eventual success, Tennant notes, was "a relentless effort to share the reasoning for sustainable investment with financial service audiences across the region: pension funds, stock market and financial service regulators, investment institutions, accountants, actuaries and so on. We explained why sustainable investment was relevant to Asia, on Asian terms. I've made concerted efforts to reach out. I think the ability to reach out is a significant feature of effective social entrepreneurs."[22]

As a result of such efforts, not only is sustainable investment in general—and areas like emission trading in particular—taking off, but there has been a parallel boom in renewable energy and so-called cleantech. Industry observers estimate that more than $70 billion of new money was invested in clean or renewable energy in 2006 alone.[23] This was more than a 40 percent improvement on the previous year, reported analyst Michael Liebreich at New Energy Finance.[24] He also noted that more than twelve hundred private equity funds were targeting environmental projects: "All the biggest private equity houses are looking at this space." As the challenges spotlighted in our ten great divides grow, these markets look set to explode, making a number of once-unreasonable people very influential and, in some cases, for better or worse, very rich.

Value and Valuation

You might think that after five hundred years of development, current methods of accounting for value creation—and destruction— are about as good as they can get. But recall Bob Massie's point that today's concepts of wealth creation are "hopelessly primitive and unsophisticated." Clearly, five hundred years of movement in one direction is no guarantee for even fifty years more. If people genuinely want to transform the capitalist system, or any other economic system, they need to consider what gets measured—which brings us to valuation.

One of the most effective champions of new ways of thinking of value has been Jed Emerson, who came up with the concept of blended value. From 1996 to 2000, he was executive director of the Roberts Enterprise Development Fund, started by George R. Roberts, founding partner of corporate raiders Kohlberg Kravis Roberts & Co. Based in the San Francisco Bay Area, Emerson worked with social entrepreneurs like Rick Aubry of Rubicon, who were trying to produce early forms of blended value.

"Traditionally," Emerson explains, "value has been understood as either economic value or social value. This has given rise to the notion that for-profit firms create economic value and nonprofit firms create social value."[25] Linked to that notion is the idea that "investments of capital are either market-rate or charitable gifts—and that firms operating to create both social and economic value are 'double bottom-line' companies, while those that are mainstream are 'single bottom-line' companies. This historical understanding of value is fundamentally wrong," he insists, "and has led to a host of social and environmental problems since, in truth, value is non-divisible."

All enterprises and corporations create blended value, he says. "The only issue up for debate is the degree to which they maximize the component elements of value, best tracked through the use of a triple bottom-line framework." But what motivated him to dig into all this in the first place? "The initial idea for attempting to map the universe of players engaged in the pursuit of economic, social and environmental value came after six weeks of seemingly endless travel in the United States and Europe," he recalls. "The [Roberts Fund] team talked to people at the heart of corporate social responsibility, social enterprise, investing, research and advocacy. And it became clear that the boom in [corporate social responsibility], human rights, sustainable development and the like has created a proliferation of silos, in the worlds of activism, government, business and investment."

Many people the team spoke to appeared to be "grappling with very similar issues and challenges, but from within their own 'silo' of orientation (whether social investing, philanthropy, social enterprise or so forth), and were largely unaware of other initiatives just 'over the wall.' " Such silos are a major issue. As Emerson puts it: "Collectively 'we' actually know much more than any 'one' of us has the bandwidth to appreciate, which led to the idea that by gathering a core representation of existing organizational and intellectual capital across all four silos of activity one might better inform specific efforts within each silo." Like the Israelites before Jericho, and like many of the people profiled in these pages, the team wondered how the silo walls might be brought down. This remains a work in progress.

Meanwhile, there is Canada's Chris Corps. He may not consider himself a social or environmental entrepreneur, but he is. He has been working to reboot international laws of asset valuation to better capture the long-term value created by buildings or infrastructure with sustainability features. He describes green valuation as "the most powerful tool you haven't yet used."[26] He also makes the point that green buildings' value is not just in their energy efficiency but in how they increase people's productivity—a notion that can switch on even the hardest-headed CFO.

So what does this mean in practice? We asked Corps for a practical example.

Last December [2006] I was asked to work with some people looking at the sewage treatment plant proposed for Greater Victoria Capital Regional District (or CRD). In June of 2007 they published their study concluding a C$1.2 billion cost for the proposed plant. In May, I was one of ten British Columbia experts and four international experts asked to a meeting with British Columbia's premier, Gordon Campbell. In July, the Cabinet approved an initial study to confirm my numbers, which I am now working on. My initial projection was that a sustainable approach could be as much as C$1.6 billion better than a traditional sewage approach. In other words a technical profit![27]

So how can the original estimates have been so wrong? "I realized that the traditional financial methods of analysis are fundamentally flawed," Corps replied.

> Basically by using a discounted cash flow they are literally discounting future value and the longer life cycle of a sustainable approach. So much so that they concluded it was unviable when the exact opposite was true. The main problem is that the traditional approach and method of both accounting and valuation analysis is what might be termed "single perspective," i.e., they only count one party's perspective. This omitted one line item alone of C\$150 million in savings from being sustainable. Re-analyzing the exact same numbers on a total cash basis over the life cycle, the difference is an amazing C\$4 billion[39] in favor of a sustainable approach. In other words, sustainability is being fundamentally failed by traditional methods.

Most strikingly, he noted that "the discounted cash flow devalued the future cost savings and value benefits, which will grow substantially over the cash flow horizon, to 2065. One hundred dollars in 2065 is only worth \$6.60 today."

Corps recognizes the importance of strategic partnerships: he is working with organizations like the International Valuation Standards Committee, Canada's Appraisal Institute, the United Kingdom's Royal Institution of Chartered Surveyors, and Mexico's Federation of Colleges, Institutes and Societies of Valuation. If he succeeds in his self-appointed task of helping demonstrate that sustainability really does add value—for example, in the projects being developed for the Beijing, Vancouver, and London Olympics—the impact could be profound. Such a mentality could influence financial institutions in ways that have proved impossible to date. And the change would help create market pull for people like ecoarchitect Bill McDonough, who has been helping companies like Ford and Nike green their factories and is also supporting China in its efforts to adopt sustainability principles as a wave of urbanization sweeps across the country.

Profound systemic change tends to be driven by new forms of transparency and accountability, by the deployment of radically new technologies, by economic discontinuities like depressions, and by major conflicts. As we have seen, however, there is another option, and that is the intervention of unreasonable people. Their ultimate success and impact will depend on the degree to which they manage to scale and replicate their solutions, a challenge we explore in chapter 7.

SEVEN

Scaling Solutions

IN THE TWENTY-PLUS YEARS since it first erupted onto the international policy and business agendas, the concept of sustainable development has become central in the public, private, and citizen sectors. Among the early flag bearers was the UN-originated Brundtland Commission with its influential report *Our Common Future*.[1] The report focused on addressing most of the ten great divides discussed in chapter 3, and the core definition of sustainable development continues to win support from leaders worldwide.[2] Still, skeptics argue that, to date, there has been a great deal more talk than action. To counter that criticism and tackle the great challenges effectively, in a timely fashion, and on a sufficient scale, we must learn how to scale and replicate the more sustainable solutions and mobilize collective effort in ways rarely seen outside of wars and space races.

Some see the challenges as staggering, and, admittedly, there are real complexities in understanding and dimensioning them. It is one of nature's paradoxes, for example, that the vast cloud of

coal smoke that hangs above China—and is visible from space—
has at least one environmental advantage, in that it is now thought
to slow the pace of global warming. One problem is partly cancel-
ing out another or, at least, slowing its advance, but there is little
room for optimism even here. China is scrambling to open new
coal mines and no fewer than five hundred new coal-fired power
stations, on top of the two thousand the country already operates.
In the process, global emissions of climate-destabilizing GHGs are
expected to jump. As such trends continue, the extent to which we
all live on one planet—and may ultimately share the same fate—
is becoming painfully clear to more people every day.

Given the success of *An Inconvenient Truth*, Al Gore's Oscar-
winning documentary on climate change, it should come as no surprise that public concern about environmental issues is rising in many
parts of the rich world. The problems in countries like China and
India, however, are on an altogether different scale. So great is the
pollution in China, for example, that four hundred thousand pre-
mature deaths are now recorded there each year because of pollution, and public pressure to clean up is building faster than many
government officials had expected.

A survey of citizens in Shanxi province—home to Datong,
China's filthy "coal capital"—found that more than 90 percent
thought that health and environmental costs are unsustainable.[3]
"If we don't protect our environment," warned Chinese environment minister Pan Yue, "our economic miracle will soon come to
an end."[4] The uncomfortable fact is that even cleaner parts of the
global economy are ill equipped to survive the twenty-first century,
let alone thrive. This conclusion is not new: it surfaces in report after
report, including the authoritative Millennium Ecosystem Assessment, which issued a "stark warning" to emphasize its finding that
"nearly two thirds of the services provided by nature to humankind
are going to be in decline worldwide."[5]

Here again, social and environmental entrepreneurs are doing
their best to wake up their fellow citizens and decision makers.
Among the handful of environmental analysts who have warned
of such trends for decades is Lester Brown. He has written or coau-

thored fifty books, which have appeared in some forty languages. Just one of those books, *Who Will Feed China?*, spawned hundreds of conferences and seminars to challenge official views on China's food prospects. Brown displays the characteristic skill of the entrepreneur: rather than simply identifying impending problems, he has mapped the market opportunities likely to result. In fact, he founded the Earth Policy Institute, aiming to provide a road map for achieving an environmentally sustainable economy.

In his book *Plan B: Rescuing a Planet Under Stress and a Civilization in Trouble* and its successor, *Plan B 2.0*, Brown mapped out the changes required for a more sustainable future.[6] His thinking spans the universe of issues that social and environmental entrepreneurs are tackling, including the stabilization of human population numbers, the universal availability of basic education, and the development of pricing mechanisms that tell the social and ecological truth—all geared to support a massive transformation to better ways of managing natural resources, like soil and freshwater, and building the hydrogen economy.

More than most, Brown acknowledges the need to scale solutions, but he is also acutely aware of how one generation's solutions can generate the next generation's problems. For example, in the biofuels sector (biofuels are plant- and animal-waste-derived alternatives to oil-based fuels), Brown has warned that the gold-rush mentality that has taken hold of investors and companies as energy security issues soar toward the top of the political agenda risks ending in the rapid spread of first-generation technologies that are, to put it mildly, unsustainable. Companies that do not already have someone like Lester Brown on their board need to plug into such people as they start to develop their own scale-up plans.

Managing the Perils of Scaling: Mitchell Kapor on the Challenge

We can learn much about the perils of scaling from the world of social and environmental entrepreneurship. Those who have studied the dynamics of scaling and replication call for "anything but a cookie-cutter process," as Jeffrey Bradach of the Bridgespan Group puts it.[7] One key factor is whether an enterprise has a strong theory of change, which uses systems thinking to map cause and effect among different parts of the system it is attempting to change. Lester Brown would readily agree. Other important success factors are the growth model that the company adopts, the market opportunity it targets, the sources of funding available to it, and the extent to which the broader business culture and operating environment catalyzes and supports entrepreneurial activity.[8] Clearly, picking the right problems to attack is critical, too: choose the wrong market or field, and scaling is much harder to accomplish.

Tapping the wisdom of someone who has been through the scaling process a number of times makes sense. Mitchell Kapor is perhaps still best known for founding Lotus Development Corporation in 1982. Later acquired by IBM, Lotus developed an early killer app: Lotus 1-2-3. Today, Kapor chairs the Open Source Applications Foundation; the Mozilla Foundation, which is evolving the Firefox Web browser; and Linden Lab, the company that came up with Second Life, a 3-D virtual world entirely built and owned by its residents (since opening to the public in 2003, Second Life's "digital continent" has attracted millions of users from around the globe).

"Scaling an organization puts stress on it," Kapor notes. "Rapid scaling of companies undergoing explosive growth—for example, Lotus, Netscape, or Google—creates damaging stress. The same is true for more recent ventures like Second Life, Mozilla, and Wikipedia . . . The latter two are nonprofits, so scaling problems are not limited to for-profit organizations. Explosive growth can happen to either a for-profit or a nonprofit in the Internet era."[9]

When asked about the challenges of scaling, other than fundraising, Kapor explains:

Every new employee who is hired has to be integrated into the organization. There are certain values, styles of behavior, and practices which are characteristic of the entity. Until a new employee learns to operate within those norms, he or she is like a foreign body introduced into an organism. The body system recognizes an alien invader and mobilizes its immune system to neutralize it. Newcomers are rendered impotent and, worse, start counterproductive efforts (infections) which have to be extinguished. The extremely rapid hiring which characterizes high-growth start-ups can ultimately overwhelm the corporate immune system, leading to breakdowns in function.

Kapor stresses:

Companies can help smooth the rapid hiring and integration process in a variety of ways, but my intuition is that there is a natural limit to the rate at which people can be added without damaging adverse effects. A second factor which complicates scaling is that when there is pressure to hire to meet the numbers, there is an inevitable tendency to lower standards and hire less qualified people who would otherwise not be brought into the organization. When the filters are too loose, it in turn introduces a new set of problems into the company by adding people whose capabilities lower the overall standard of performance.

But what about companies that already operate on a large global scale, like BP, GE, Toyota, and Wal-Mart? Kapor is skeptical about their potential to progress toward anything like sustainability, though he stresses that "change is always possible, and there is nothing dishonorable about beginning with baby steps. In fact, it takes a lot of courage. But it's not an accident that most businesses only get serious about social responsibility after some sort of crisis . . . At such times, the prospect of acknowledging difficult realities in order to begin to change them seems like it might even be the better end of a bargain. Of course," he notes, "once the crisis passes, it is incredibly easy to slip back into complacency."

Therefore, to promote scalability for social and environmental ventures and their partnerships with mainstream businesses, we need a number of ingredients. These include a universal environmental—and, eventually, triple-bottom-line—accounting language to help businesses monitor progress; the evolution and deployment of professional skills in such areas as monitoring, impact assessment, auditing, reporting, and assurance; market incentives that track and punish or reward corporate performance; and back-up public sector processes that create an overall sense of direction and ensure enforcement. Much progress has been made on all these fronts, particularly in developed countries, but one of the most critical missing links is a universally accepted accounting language that would assess the extent to which all enterprises—whatever their scale—were heading toward sustainability.

Accounting for Sustainability: WWF and One Planet Business

As we noted in chapter 6, to understand and address social and environmental challenges, organizations first need appropriate systems to measure and account for their activities. One promising initiative is the One Planet Business accounting method under development by WWF and its partners. (WWF stands for World Wide Fund for Nature around the world except for North America, where it is known as World Wildlife Fund.) There are many competing attempts to set universal accounting standards, and One Planet Business is among the leading contenders. It promises to help business leaders and others measure their impact on the environment and pin down the detailed steps they need to take toward environmental sustainability. Just as Samuel Plimsoll campaigned to ensure that ships were marked with lines showing how deep they could be laded and remain safe to sail in, such pioneers are trying to work out how to draw a line around the planet to help its growing crew navigate the new century without foundering.

The impetus for One Planet Business and similar initiatives has its roots in the 1980s, when business leaders started to awaken to the new sustainable development agenda. There were limited ways to measure environmental impact at the time, so, as WWF's One

Planet Business study puts it, "unnoticed, humanity's overall eco-logical footprint—that is, the resources required to meet global consumption—for the first time exceeded the planet's biocapacity, or the carrying capacity of its ecological systems."[10]

In the new century, however, we know that:

We are in a situation of "overshoot" where consumption exceeds long-term supply by approximately 23 percent. In other words, it takes one year and three months to regenerate what humanity uses within a given year. This overshoot is only possible because much of the natural resource capital base has accumulated over time. This is as true for stocks of renewable resources—such as soils, forests, and underground aquifers—as it is for essentially non-renewable resources like oil and natural gas. By drawing down stocks of natural capital, consumption can temporarily exceed ecological limits. Just as personal expenses can be greater than income for a period, we can operate on "ecological credit." However, the longer the overshoot continues, the greater the like-lihood that the regenerative capacity of the planet's ecosystems will be degraded.[11]

WWF concludes:

On current evidence and trends, there is virtually no prospect of moving back into ecological surplus. Resource use is accelerating. World energy demand, for example, has been increasing twice as fast since 2000 (at 2.6 percent per annum) as it did in the pre-vious decade, and with the astonishing growth of the emerging economies, rates of resource use can be expected to accelerate further. Projecting the impacts of these trajectories on the econ-omy's overall ecological footprint suggests that, even at moder-ate rates of growth, the equivalent of 1.5 planets will be needed to meet demand by 2020 and 2.3 planets by 2030. This situa-tion has become today's decisive *environmental* challenge, and is fast becoming tomorrow's critical *economic* challenge.[12]

WWF and One Planet Business plan to work with a series of industry sectors—beginning with the automobile industry and moving on to such areas as food, housing, and power generation—to calculate what share of the planet's resources can be afforded for each particular activity and to develop strategies for capturing the new market opportunities that will arise. WWF notes, "No one player has a complete grasp of the problem, much less the full range of potential solutions. Making real and enduring progress depends on assembling all of the key players in a 'systems change network' and collectively working toward shared goals."[13] So the intention is to build the One Planet Business network, sector by sector, starting with those that have the most impact. Future-oriented sectors and their investors probably ought to lobby for inclusion sooner rather than later.

Raising Great Stinks: Jack Sim and WTO

Initiatives like One Planet Business will solve problems only if they can be replicated and scaled fast enough. And, as we have already emphasized, politics will be at the pumping heart of the transition, often propelled by "great stinks"—where major pollution problems force the unwilling hands of politicians—and major controversies. To explore the possibilities of replication and scaling, let's take a sector not yet flagged by the WWF initiative: sewerage. Few things symbolize the breakdown of civilization so powerfully as the absence of functional toilets. Indeed, getting toilets in place— or working again—is one of the first steps in any model 1 emergency response to a major disaster like the 2004 Asian tsunami or Hurricane Katrina.

Social entrepreneur Jack Sim recognized that much of the problem with addressing the lack of clean public toilets around the world lay in the taboo nature of the subject. So, like Mechai Viravaidya, the Thai entrepreneur who uses humor to promote condom use, Sim has used a light touch in approaching a tricky subject. For one thing, he named his organization the World Toilet Organization (WTO).

Sim has mastered the art of media leverage and has established, among other things, a World Toilet Day. "Let's all take a few moments to observe this very special occasion," quipped Dave Barry, a syndicated columnist based at the *Miami Herald* who wrote about World Toilet Day, "and then let's wash our hands!"[14] It is hard to believe that with a mere $250,000 a year (WTO is truly a leveraged nonprofit), Sim has been able to organize five world summits that each brought together some four hundred participants from twenty-five countries. He has also convinced governments and corporations to compete for the privilege of being the country with the cleanest public toilets. Through his operational arm in Singapore, he has come up with the Happy Toilet star rating program, which rewards the best public toilets in the city-state based on design, quality, and maintenance criteria. A similar initiative in the United Kingdom, the Loo of the Year Awards, replicated the Singapore program. Meanwhile, to advance research and development, Sim has spearheaded the World Toilet College in collaboration with Singapore Polytechnic, introducing courses in restroom design, restroom maintenance, and sanitation.

Why is this important? One reason is that more than half of the developing world's population has no access to decent toilets. According to the UN, more than 5 million children die every year from sanitation-related diseases such as diarrhea. In India and China alone, a billion people without sanitary facilities relieve themselves on streets and in rivers, polluting river water, which large numbers of people use for drinking water. Human feces are the biggest culprit in water contamination. And even where there are public toilets, they are very often poorly maintained.

According to WTO, the average person visits the toilet twenty-five hundred times a year, about six times a day. Amazingly, no less than three years of the average lifespan are spent in the toilet. Moreover, if you are a woman, you spend three times longer in toilets than the average man. No one has calculated the size of the global toilet industry, as far as we know, but since restrooms and related infrastructure account for about 7 percent of total construction costs, the value of the industry is probably in the tens of billions of dollars.

This is where the issue of scaling really comes in. Take London, credited with building the world's first modern sewer, in the mid-nineteenth century. The city was suffering from recurring—and devastating—cholera epidemics. In 1853–1854, more than ten thousand Londoners were killed by the disease.[15] The turning point came in the hot summer of 1858, the year of the "Great Stink," which overwhelmed all those who went near the Thames, including those in Parliament. Finally, enough pressure mounted, and legislation was passed enabling work to begin on new sewers and related improvements. By 1866, most of London was connected to an ambitious and well-executed sewer network devised by the great engineer Joseph Bazalgette.

Toilets are important, no doubt. Beijing, for example, planned to spend $100 million to create about thirty-seven hundred world-class toilets in time for its 2008 Summer Olympics. And WTO has supported the creation of a star-rating system for Beijing's lavatories. China says that it also will build millions of low-cost toilets in rural areas over the coming decades. On an even bigger scale, China and other emerging nations are making substantial investments in sewage plants and environmentally friendly technologies. So just as the world needs Jack Sims, as countries like China create ever-bigger local, regional, and global stinks, the world also needs a new generation of Bazalgettes to clean up its megacities—and even to design sustainable new cities from scratch. When such people emerge, they may strike others as unreasonable for a decade or two, but in the end, the successful ones will not only drive revolutionary jumps in living standards but will also create huge new economic opportunity spaces.

Seizing Large-Scale Opportunities: GE

No matter how far and fast Jack Sim is able to expand WTO's activities, it probably would take him decades to reach an annual turnover of $1 billion. True, that is not WTO's purpose—rather, it acts as a catalyst to help others scale their ventures. It innovates, tests, refines, and implements in ways that mainstream companies can't or won't. Scaling on a truly meaningful level, however, will require input from mainstream businesses.

One giant company that has its eyes on China is GE. With its history of polychlorinated biphenyl pollution in the Hudson River, among other things, the old GE would not have readily come to mind as an innovator in sustainable development. But then Jeffrey Immelt succeeded Jack Welch as CEO. Whereas Welch was notoriously hard nosed on issues like the environment, Immelt caught the world's attention by shifting all of GE's businesses toward a culture of creativity and imagination.

An early signal that things were changing came when GE agreed to clean up the chemicals in the Hudson—at least to the degree that current technology permits. That, however, wasn't even the most striking change. Senior GE executives were told that every business unit would have to meet strict targets for cutting GE's overall carbon dioxide and GHG emissions by at least 1 percent from their 2004 levels before 2012. If this sounds less than demanding, consider that, otherwise, the company's projected revenue growth to 2012 would have boosted its GHG emissions by 40 percent above 2004 levels.[16]

In addition, with his Ecomagination initiative (with the mantra "green is green"), Immelt pledged to create huge new revenues from environmental markets. "The company vows to double its revenues from 17 clean-technology businesses," the *Economist* reported, "ranging from renewable energy and hydrogen fuel cells, to water filtration and purification systems, to cleaner aircraft and locomotive engines. This would take such products from $10 billion in sales in 2004 to $20 billion by 2010, with more ambitious targets thereafter. To get there, Immelt has promised to double research spending on clean products, from $700 million per year to $1.5 billion, by 2010."[17] On the wind-energy front, GE has been seeing a marked increase in orders and predicts that sales will soon exceed $4 billion a year. John Krenicki, head of GE's energy division, also has high hopes for the company's "clean coal" power technology. He is aiming to boost annual sales of cleaner coal-gasification systems from less than $500 million to between $4 billion and $5 billion over the next decade.[18]

The Ecomagination initiative differs from most corporate responsibility programs because GE is determined to make serious profits from it. In the first two years of operation, Ecomagination revenues doubled to $12 billion, and orders in the pipeline jumped from $17 billion to $50 billion—big numbers even for such a giant company. One Goldman Sachs investment banker noted, "Every one of the Ecomagination initiatives looks commercially viable, even without the green angle."[19] But given that some of the company's customers—for instance, customers in the power generation sector—are dead-set against this transition, isn't GE at risk of alienating those on whom its very future depends? "This is not just GE jamming environment down their throats," insisted GE Vice Chairman David Calhoun.[20] He explained that GE had decided that environmental responsibility is something sensible customers will eventually want and concluded, "Let's stop putting our heads in the sand, dodging environmental interests, and go from defense to [offense]."

Skeptics note that other major companies—including chemical producers like Dow and DuPont, energy groups like BP, and water companies like SUEZ—tried to dive into the green space in the 1980s and 1990s, offering a wide range of environmental services. Many had predicted double-digit growth, and some invested heavily in developing-country markets. Although the markets did grow, the risk proved higher—and the profitability lower—than expected. As a result, by the late 1990s, many of these companies had scaled back their investments. While the *Economist* noted that GE is better positioned than many of those early entrants, "given its deep pockets and top-level commitment to the approach," the magazine also cautioned that any "forecast of endlessly fast growth should be treated with caution."[21]

For one thing, profit margins in countries like India and China are often tight, even if they are where analysts expect some 60 percent of GE's revenue growth to come from in the coming decade. On a more positive note, some predict that China could become a "green lab" as its problems mount.[22] Another word of encouragement: Chinese president Hu Jintao recently called for Asian Pacific leaders to join the country in developing a clean, resource-conserving "circular economy."[23]

The magic ingredient in GE's Ecomagination venture, meanwhile, is likely to be creativity, not one of the company's traditional strengths. The Six Sigma culture ingrained in GE by Jack Welch "frowned on deviations from the plan," noted Lorraine Bolsinger, head of Ecomagination. That old culture will no doubt have to change to suit the fast-paced markets GE is now diving into. "Jeff is asking us to take a really big swing," Bolsinger said. The mantra for Ecomagination? "Fail early, fail fast," Bolsinger explained and added, "This is hard for us."[24] But as such pioneers and early adopters learn how to raise their game by diving into tomorrow's nascent markets, the task of catching up is likely to become progressively harder for key competitors.

Managing at the Edge:
The Importance of Pioneering Investors

One way to make it easier for the business community overall is to let the unreasonable people take the early strain, cope with the inevitable failures, and share the lessons of success. This is one of many reasons why we should be grateful to the philanthropists and foundations that back leading social and environmental entrepreneurs. For example, Stephan Schmidheiny, profiled in the introduction, has been a major investor in Solarcentury. Founded by Jeremy Leggett, originally head of research at Greenpeace UK, the company started out with £6 million (about $12 million) from Schmidheiny and received an additional £1 million (about $2 million) from Scottish and Southern Energy, after which Leggett moved to open out his funding sources.[25]

Solarcentury's biggest project to date has involved equipping the Co-operative Insurance Society (CIS) tower in Manchester, England, with some seven thousand photovoltaic solar collectors. These should generate 180,000 units of renewable energy a year, which CIS—with an eye to both national tastes and the media—estimates would make 9 million cups of tea. On the nature of the job, Leggett speaks for many social and environmental entrepreneurs in saying, "It sounds like a cliché, but it is a thrill. You're trying to manage at the edge."[26]

A growing sense of urgency is helping draw new investors to the sustainability agenda. In the United Kingdom during 2006, for example, property magnate Vincent Tchenguiz—originally from Iran—announced plans to invest £1 billion ($2 billion) in environmental ventures, an outgrowth of his work with more than fifty such businesses.[27] Virgin's Sir Richard Branson also joined the ranks of global-warming activists that same year by committing $3 billion to tackle climate change. The billionaire pledged all profits from his Virgin air and rail interests over the next decade to combating rising global temperatures. The money will not go to charities but will be invested in a new branch (called Virgin Fuels) of Branson's ever-expanding Virgin conglomerate. Much of the investment is slated to go to work on biofuels.

The quality of entrepreneurs operating in these spaces is improving all the time. "We are seeing a very high caliber of entrepreneur coming through now, many of them people who have done this before with other companies," says Nicholas Parker of the Cleantech Venture Network.[28] "This is a quantum leap better than the entrepreneurs we were seeing in this space four or five years ago." One key shift is in the way these people view the challenge. Earlier generations of green entrepreneur had a "save the world mentality," Parker recalls. "This is not necessarily a bad thing, but they tended not to bring entrepreneurial rigor or discipline or the return on investment ethos." Even those early entrepreneurs who did manage to create successful businesses sometimes had trouble working with outside investors (see the sidebar, "To Sell or Not to Sell?").

To Sell or Not to Sell?

ONE OF the toughest moments any entrepreneur faces is considering whether to sell out. One of us was at the Ben & Jerry's board meeting when founders Ben Cohen and Jerry Greenfield decided they would have to sell out. It was an excruciating period for them. If the social enterprise sector is to work well as an incubator of future businesses, however, the mechanisms of investments, mergers, and acquisitions have to be considered.

One of the first social entrepreneurs—we didn't use the term then—we came across in our careers was Andrew Whitley. Originally the BBC's Russia correspondent, Whitley and his then wife created the Village Bakery in Cumbria, in northern England, in 1976. They were very unusual because they based their entire business on organic methods, renewable energy, and artisanal techniques. The real challenges began when a major supermarket chain discovered the Village Bakery in 1991. We asked Whitley whether selling out was always part of his business plan. "I didn't have a business plan," he replied. "Indeed, I didn't know what one was for the first ten years of my business career. I had no particular endgame in mind. The decision to sell was, in effect, taken for me when my ex-wife indicated that she wanted to leave the partnership, both business and personal. So the choice was between giving up the whole thing and selling enough of it to generate some cash while allowing me to remain in the business."[a]

There followed a long search for investors who showed any inkling of what the business was about. Whitley eventually found three people who did, the folk behind the successful Phineas Fogg brand, and they acquired 66 percent of the shares. "But then they were bought out—pretty much over my head—by a local bakery, Bells, in 1998, with my share dropping to 24.9 percent," he recalled. "The second stage, 2001–2002, involved a difficult negotiation in which it seemed that the majority shareholder wanted to engineer my exit for nothing. I took legal advice and consulted people like

Rachel Rowlands of Rachel's Dairy, Lizzie Vann of Organix Brands, and Craig Sams of Whole Earth and Green & Black's."

So what advice would Whitley give to a would-be social entrepreneur today? "Find a way of achieving adequate capitalization before you start," he said, "so you can cushion against temporary dips in profitability caused by a determination to stick to your principles."

The options to raise needed capital include angel investors (as with the three investors behind Phineas Fogg and, in some cases, a superphilanthropist or two); a trade sale (as was the case for Bells); a management buyout; or an IPO to begin the process of taking the company public.

To get a better sense of how trade sales can operate, we talked to Craig Sams, who had been one of Andrew Whitley's advisers. Sams has sold two social enterprises: Whole Earth, now part of Kallo Foods, and organic chocolate makers Green & Black's, now part of Cadbury. We asked him whether selling out was always part of the game plan. "Yes," he replied, "but previous attempts hadn't been successful. We offered Whole Earth to Heinz in 1996, thinking it the perfect opportunity for them. But they went with their own brand. The decision to sell Green & Black's became inevitable when venture investors William Kendall and Nick Beart made an offer of cash and shares retention. Encouraged by my father and my wife [Josephine Fairley, cofounder of Green & Black's], I agreed, and we were into the venture capital stage. Everyone had invested in a business plan that showed an exit in five years or so."

When asked about the benefits of being part of Cadbury, Sams said, "We have long leveraged the production and processing powers of others, but now with Cadbury, we have the global reach of a multinational and can make strategic decisions without being constrained by short-term cost issues." Would he have sold to any interested company? Nestlé, for example? No, Sams replied, uneasily aware of the giant Swiss company's poor reputation. "I'd have had to have plastic surgery and gone to live in Uzbekistan if it had been Nestlé!"

We also asked Sams whether he had any advice for early-stage social entrepreneurs. "Same advice as Andrew," he said. "Capital is wonderful stuff. I was always constrained by being undercapitalized and used each successful product as a cash cow to fund the next. Whole Earth peanut butter, for example, was what kept Green & Black's going in the early days."

Finally, we spoke to a social entrepreneur who had recently gone through an IPO process: Rory Stear of Freeplay Energy. We asked him how he saw the options as he thought about scaling up. He explained:

Unlike many other social entrepreneurs, we always intended to seek external investment and, eventually, to take the business public. In the early days, we had sold slices of the business to investors like Anita and Gordon Roddick and the GE Pension Trust. Any investor wants to know what [his or her] exit is going to be. Our problem was that our first-round investors were tired, and over the years, we had developed an impossibly complicated capital structure, with some investors effectively having the power of veto on what we did. The IPO helped straighten that out. And it's an unfortunate fact of business life that often the people who make the real money out of a business are the second-round investors.

What advice would Rory Stear offer to a would-be social entrepreneur? "I agree with Andrew and Craig," he said. "Try to make sure you have enough capital from the outset, or you end up being driven by the deals."

a. This and all other quotations in this story are from John Elkington, "To Sell or Not to Sell?" *SustainAbility Radar*, September 2005, 8–11.

The Cleantech Group of investors (which includes the Cleantech Venture Network) is building a powerful platform for environmental entrepreneurs and ventures. It estimates that between 1999 and 2006, more than $8.3 billion was invested in cleantech deals in North America alone, with the continent's demand for such capital predicted to average $3.9 billion a year between 2006 and 2009. The current pace of deal making, Parker explained in 2006, put cleantech ahead of the semiconductor sector—and just about level with telecoms. Also, there is now a much stronger presence of venture capitalists at Cleantech Group events, including leading firms like Kleiner Perkins Caufield & Byers (KPCB).

Although the initial $100 million that KPCB earmarked for cleantech—part of a $600 million fund dedicated to IT, life sciences, and medical devices—won't save the world anytime soon, it was an early signal of the importance leading venture capitalists are placing on this area. And those venture capitalists' voices are influential: where they go, others follow. In parallel, their lobbying activities could make a real difference with politicians who are keen to attract and support the entrepreneurs of the future. In fact, two top KPCB partners—John Denniston and John Doerr—note that one of today's biggest challenges is that we don't yet have enough of the kind of political leaders the future deserves, "who have the courage not to invade Iraq but to impose a [U.S.] gas tax."[29] So can we expect KPCB to lobby for the necessary political changes to get cleantech fully up and running? "We have been politically active," Denniston noted, "and we'll see a lot more of that."[30]

If Jeremy Leggett, Stephan Schmidheiny, Vincent Tchenguiz, Richard Branson, Nicholas Parker, John Denniston, John Doerr, and other apparently unreasonable people are successful in redirecting the political debate in this way, the world may have a much better array of choices for the future social, environmental, and economic environment. We turn to those choices in our concluding chapter.

Lessons for Tomorrow's Leaders

R ECALL FOR A MOMENT the inspiration for our title: "The reasonable man adapts himself to the world," George Bernard Shaw said, whereas "the unreasonable one persists in trying to adapt the world to himself. Therefore all progress depends on the unreasonable man."[1] We have spotlighted an array of people who were— and, in many cases, still are—dubbed "unreasonable." One reason they are considered unreasonable is that the rest of us find it difficult to see radical disruptions coming, whether those disruptions promise breakthrough or could create an economic, social, or environmental breakdown.

Let's take just one example. In *The Long Emergency*, James Howard Kunstler warns of dire outcomes for societies that are overly dependent on the dwindling supplies of easily accessible oil.[2] For instance, he predicts the end—indeed, the collapse—of American suburbia as energy prices soar in the post-peak-oil era. "We have invested all our wealth in a living arrangement with no future," he argues. "In building suburbia, we embarked on the greatest misallocation of wealth in the history of the world." Instead of ghost towns, expect ghost suburbs and exurbs.

Unreasonable? On most current assumptions, yes, but many social entrepreneurs have seen with their own eyes what happens when governance, economic, social, or ecological systems break down. Many of the entrepreneurs in this book—among them, Fazle Abed of BRAC, Bunker Roy of Barefoot College, Muhammad Yunus of the Grameen Group, Andrea and Barry Coleman of Riders for Health—had their epiphanies when confronted by brute catastrophe.

The CIA has predicted that environmental pressures will exacerbate global tensions and increase the risks of conflict in the coming decade.[3] Social and environmental entrepreneurs, however, believe that such a tide can be diverted—and even turned. Take the desperate plight of the world's coral reef ecosystems and marine fisheries—and the work of the Marine Stewardship Council (MSC). An independent, global hybrid nonprofit organization based in London, the MSC aims to reverse the decline in the world's fisheries. It seeks to harness consumer purchasing power to generate change and promote environmentally responsible stewardship of the world's most important renewable food source.

How does the MSC plan to accomplish this? It has developed an environmental standard for well-managed, sustainable fisheries. Like other certification bodies, it uses a product label to reward good practice. The MSC was first established by Unilever (at the time, the world's largest buyer of seafood) and WWF in 1997 and has been operating independently since 1999. WWF's involvement was itself an indication of the way in which the NGO world has been developing innovative partnerships with leading companies to mutate markets. The MSC has succeeded in bringing together a broad coalition of supporters from over a hundred organizations in more than twenty countries. CEO Rupert Howes notes that convincing retailers like Wal-Mart of the need to specify, stock, and promote sustainable fish has been a major shot in the arm for the MSC and the agenda it champions.

In the end, however, even such powerful partnerships will not save the world's fisheries, let alone its oceanic ecosystems. For that to happen, it needs effective global governance mechanisms and sustained political will.

How to Build the Power

We conclude with some guidance on what others can do to help support the work of these game changers, change makers, and social and environmental entrepreneurs. We also offer a number of takeaways for tomorrow's leaders.

Focus on Scalable, Entrepreneurial Solutions

The time has come to refocus on creativity, innovation, and scale—all aspects of entrepreneurial solutions to the great challenges of the future. Happily, the potential for breakthrough solutions is considerable and growing. It's true that such entrepreneurship is not a new phenomenon, but its building momentum offers one of the most hopeful signals that we may achieve something like sustainable development in this century.

Tackle Apparently Insoluble Problems

It takes courage to attempt the apparently impossible, but throughout history, the great innovators and entrepreneurs—like those profiled here—have embraced such challenges. As we've asserted throughout this book, there are lessons to be learned in how these people see the future, how they connect the dots to solve seemingly insoluble problems, how they often dive in without thinking about how to make a profit from their enterprise, how they try to measure the immeasurable, and how they work to change political, governance, social, and economic systems to combat wider dysfunctions.

Be Prepared to Fail—but Learn from the Failures

No matter how unreasonable, visionary, pragmatic, and lucky an entrepreneur might be, shaping and carrying out a transformational initiative is the result of trial and error. Almost no one gets it right the first time. Entrepreneurs who dream big must be prepared for setbacks, even of the fall-flat-on-their-face variety. Unfortunately, some societies punish failures more than others; such cultures are more risk averse and less entrepreneurial. Independent of the cultural context in which they occur, all failures bruise egos. Still, they can be invaluable inputs to future success. The most important thing is to regroup and head toward the goal.

Experiment with New Business Models

Despite their prominence in the management literature, business model innovations can be hard to achieve. For one thing, it's tough to think of alternatives to the status quo. That's why tomorrow's leaders should explore what social and environmental entrepreneurs are doing—and attempting.

More than anything else, successful social and environmental entrepreneurs demonstrate the urgent need to be pragmatic when facing huge challenges, adopting nonprofit, for-profit, or hybrid business models to suit the context. Our chapter 1 discussion of the three main models used by leading entrepreneurs underscores the fact that all those models create multiple forms of value, whether or not today's markets reward them for doing so. We have spotlighted many model 1 (leveraged nonprofit ventures) enterprises, noting that model 2 (hybrid nonprofit ventures) is where the most interesting efforts are focused. In the long run, however, model 3 (social business ventures) offers the greatest opportunity for scaling and replication.

Close the Pay Gap

Everyday it seems as if we learn of a different gap between the haves and have-nots. But one gap that rarely makes headlines—the salary gap between commercial and social enterprises—remains the elephant in the room, curtailing the capacity of model 1, 2, and 3 social ventures to achieve long-term success and viability. Why the disinterest in this particular gap? Perhaps because it is considered to be a matter of individual career choice. The truth, however, is that social entrepreneurship will only succeed if the relevant enterprises have quality employees. Talented individuals of all ages may seek to dedicate themselves to organizations that are "fundamentally innovative, morally compelling and philosophically positive." That goal, however, should not come at the sacrifice of earning a decent salary.[4]

Currently, even the most successful social ventures struggle to attract and keep top talent, and that difficulty threatens every aspect of these organizations' ability to grow and have a wider impact. While the motivation to join a social enterprise is rarely (if ever) financial, investors—including individuals, foundations, and corporations—can have a huge impact on leveling the playing field by creating compensatory salary mechanisms that bring social venture remuneration on par with market rates.

Join Forces

Whatever their rhetoric about changing the world, these entrepreneurs know that they cannot succeed on their own. Even if they scaled at the rate that businesses like Amazon, eBay, or Google managed, most would still make only a small dent in the overall problems they are trying to address. As we saw with the MSC, they need partners that are able to do the heavy lifting.

Money remains the key headache for most of these people, whether their enterprises are nonprofit or for-profit. Typically, these entrepreneurs did not pick particular challenges because they were likely (or unlikely) to be profitable but because they represent market failures. Chapter 2 spotlighted a number of routes to money and other resources that these people take, but a huge wave of financial innovation is needed to help the emerging entrepreneurial solutions achieve their social and market potential.

Seed Tomorrow's Markets

If the needs of 7 billion to 10 billion people are to be met effectively, equitably, and sustainably, vast new markets will need to be created, financed, and regulated. Chapter 3 explored the great divides that stop this from happening today and may offer new prospects for tomorrow. Given the role of experimentation in finding long-term solutions, social and environmental entrepreneurs can make a critical contribution by testing out new models and technologies in relatively low-risk ways—in the process, helping seed tomorrow's markets.

Feed Growing Expectations

Nobelist Muhammad Yunus put it well when he spoke of "bonsai people"—and of the need to create new opportunity spaces for billions of people around the world. Chapter 4 investigated some of the market failures that keep billions of people from achieving their full potential. A key requirement in correcting such failures is to help people believe that a better world is possible. Access, price, and quality are among the dimensions leading entrepreneurs address in tackling that challenge, but they need help from many other sectors of society.

One potential source of longer-term support is business retirees—including Sweden's controversial Percy Barnevik, who by 2007 had invested around $14 million in Hand in Hand, which uses microfinance to support entrepreneurs in India. Within five years, he aims to create 1.3 million jobs and 250,000 businesses in the state of Tamil Nadu alone.[5] His five-pillar model, with which he hopes to create 50 million jobs worldwide over the next decade, is based on mobilizing illiterate women, eliminating child labor, improving water and waste management, and equipping citizens with the basic tools of democracy.

Help Democratize Technology

Technology's role is often overestimated in the short term, but it can be decisive in the long term. The principles of the open source movement can help align technology with the values and priorities of wider civil society. As the saying goes, "Nobody is as smart as everybody."[6] So let people in. Chapter 5 focused on efforts to democratize four clusters of entrepreneurial work, from basic building blocks like bricks to the tools of biotechnology. Each of these areas both benefits from and extends the reach of the open source approach.

Work to Change the System

Although public and private sector leaders alike will probably argue that changing the system is the realm of folk like Marx and Lenin, the fact is that social and environmental entrepreneurs' work casts a hard light on the current economic system's dysfunctions. Chapter 6 showed that the truly powerful unreasonable people are unwilling to settle for palliative half measures. Instead, time and again, they push for systemic change in the institutions that shape markets—and for solutions that will scale and become sustainable and equitable.

Figure Out How to Scale and Replicate

Even the perfect solution to a great global—or local—problem will create little or no value unless it can be scaled and replicated in good time and at reasonable cost. Some of our entrepreneurs already understand this element of the equation, and others need to learn it, as discussed in chapter 7. Scalability is one reason why so many of these people are keen to build partnerships with mainstream businesses and financial institutions. The role of governments is crucial here, too: Bill Dunster's zero-carbon architecture at Britain's BedZed ecohousing development is a great example.[7] BedZed is the country's largest green housing project, offering just eighty-two housing units; its biggest impact, however, may be that it inspired British prime minister Gordon Brown to announce five new ecotowns, with a hundred thousand ecohomes, designed along similar lines.

Within Reason, Cultivate the Art of Being Unreasonable

Unreasonable entrepreneurs may be hard acts to follow, but their perspectives on tomorrow's social needs, market opportunities, business models, and leadership styles are important in both the public and private sectors, as well as to all citizens who value the earth's natural, social, and financial resources. As a minimum, leaders in the public, private, and citizen sectors should visit some of their own country's leading social entrepreneurs, with a view to seeing how they can help leverage change and to learn how to reboot their own thinking and behaviors. How about inviting leading social and environmental entrepreneurs into your strategic conversations with key external stakeholders and even onto your board?

How Can Others Help?

Opening up existing institutions and power centers to entrepreneurs is important, but it won't scale at the rates that the great social and environmental divides demand. To get a better grip on the sort of support the entrepreneurs themselves thought would be needed, we carried out an electronic survey of several hundred leading social entrepreneurs and those who are trying to help them from the realms of government, business, and finance. We uncovered several ways that others can support the entrepreneurs' work:[8]

- Government, in all its forms, attracted the highest score for its support and potential impact. Only rarely do social entrepreneurs go directly into politics and government (exceptions include Kenya's Wangari Maathai and France's Bernard Kouchner, who cofounded Médecins Sans Frontières and was appointed by President Nicolas Sarkozy as foreign minister). Elsewhere, they must rely on politicians and government officials. So what do they want these people to do? Among the actions respondents called for are improved tax incentives for social entrepreneurship, innovative financial instruments to encourage banks and pension funds to get involved, stronger property rights, simplified regulation, and incentives to encourage public sector employees to remove barriers to innovation and entrepreneurship.

- Bilateral and multilateral institutions have key roles to play in increasing transparency, stimulating entrepreneurial cultures, raising awareness of social entrepreneurship, expanding the use of public-private partnerships, and supporting the necessary expert studies.

- Business and financial institutions should redefine their corporate giving to include not just money but also access to crucial strategic, technical, and managerial assets and skills. They also need to wake up to entrepreneurs' potential as a source of market intelligence, on-the-ground experience, and novel hybrid business models. Business and financial institutions need to be financially innovative and boost the flow of capital available through community development institutions, funds of funds, social venture funds, the creative use of secondary markets, and tax-exempt bonds. In other cases, strategic partnerships will be key, like the one that Solarcentury has formed with Sony to manufacture solar electric roof tiles in Wales. Solarcentury expects to make $8 million worth of tiles in 2007–2008, a figure it hopes to jump to $140 million by 2011–2012, which is where the Sony deal will be mission-critical.

- Free of some of the tyrannies of the voting booth and the bottom line, foundations and other philanthropic institutions can be crucial sources not just of funding but also of disciplined innovation, the ability to spot and groom talent, and patient persistence as entrepreneurs experiment and, often, fail. Respondents encouraged these funders to offer patience, persistence, and consistency in their support. Survey responders also invited these institutions to standardize and simplify the various reporting requirements they impose on those they support. Foundations and other funders should also foster systemic change by helping reform social capital markets.

- Educational institutions are vital for the long-term success of communities, countries, and the global economy. While not everyone is cut out to be an entrepreneur, educational institutions can teach the skills that propel world-class entrepreneurs. They therefore need to cultivate entrepreneurial thinking, promote interdisciplinary programs, provide internships and other opportunities to expose young people to the world of entrepreneurship, stimulate the formation of national and global networks, contribute research to the field, and support young entrepreneurs with awards.

How Can Entrepreneurs Help Themselves and Each Other?

In the same survey, we asked entrepreneurs what they themselves can do to increase their chances of success. In reverse order of importance, from least to most important, here are their replies.

First, they felt that they could do more to increase solidarity and mentoring in their own community and work with networks and intermediaries. Second, they acknowledged that they need to do more to ensure smooth and effective successions when they move

to new ventures. Third, they recognized tl
to help frame the challenges and opport
plain how they can help. Fourth, they
portance of building effective strategic a
with the public, private, and civil society
that their organizations needed to embrac
tures, accountability, transparency, and
ment. And sixth, which was equally rar
they stressed the fundamental need to ch:
sets and thinking on the timetables for p

We hope *The Power of Unreasonab*
preneurs' voices, thinking, and achievem
new—audience. These people exhibit a
Arthur Schopenhauer defined it. "Talent
can hit," he noted, but "genius hits a tar
This skill will become more critical as v
twenty-first century. As the challenges gr
able to remain optimistic about the long
work of the innovators and entrepreneu:
encourages us to embrace the notion th
the impossible takes a little longer.

Where Do Unreasonable Entrepreneurs Cluster?

WHERE CAN WE FIND social entrepreneurs? The answer is everywhere, although certain countries and regions tend to turn up more than their fair share. When, a few years ago, we analyzed the list of Schwab Foundation entrepreneurs, a rough head count showed the continents falling into the following sequence, from the most entrepreneurs to the least: Asia, Latin America, North America, Africa, and Europe.[1]

The greatest concentration of Asian social entrepreneurs is found in the Indian subcontinent. Three countries of the four in the region—India, Pakistan, and Bangladesh—are well represented. There are many reasons for this high level of activity, including the political problems that the region has suffered since its partition in the 1940s, the sheer scale of the poverty-related dilemmas that have dogged these countries, and the extraordinary number of natural disasters that have affected them—including the tsunami of late 2004.

Next stop, Latin America. Again, there are many reasons why social entrepreneurship has taken root in the region. Apart from population pressures, widespread poverty, and growing environmental problems, governments there have historically been weak, corrupt, and ineffective. To try to fill the vacuum, many of the churches in these countries have encouraged entrepreneurial solutions to social problems. If you run down the Schwab Foundation's worldwide list of outstanding entrepreneurs, the largest number from any single country outside the United States (with twenty) comes from Brazil (with nine).

It may seem surprising, given the economic wealth of North America overall, to learn that the United States had the most number of social entrepreneurs in the Schwab Foundation listing, but the facts speak for themselves. You find such entrepreneurs everywhere in the United States, from the high-tech world of Silicon Valley to the many Native American reservations and their sometimes third world living conditions. An example of the latter is the First Nations Development Institute, founded by Rebecca Adamson, a Cherokee, which has spearheaded a cultural paradigm shift in Native American communities, encouraging entrepreneurship instead of passivity. It's true that many American social entrepreneurs target the rest of the world's problems, but a surprising number are also focusing on homegrown issues. They include people working to support the growing numbers of elderly as well as those fighting to protect the interests of independent workers, from nannies and taxi drivers to software designers and consultants.

It is a big jump, in several senses, from North America to Africa. The second-largest continent, Africa is often seen as the most troubled, even a basket case. The region's problems have many roots and many aggravating factors. Some are a legacy of the colonial era. Others are a result of later meddling by previous (and would-be) colonial powers, the stupefying social and economic impacts of diseases like HIV/AIDS, or Africa's own failings, like the pervasive corruption found in its countries. Many social entrepreneurs in the region, including Kenya's Wangari Maathai, have had to fight corruption and even political tyranny.

The second-smallest continent, Europe, also has its heroes of social enterprise. For a long time Europe was overshadowed by the rapid evolution of the United States and the Soviet Union, but now it is on the rise, with the eastward expansion of the European Union well on the way to creating the world's biggest political and economic region. Given that fact, you might think that the continent would be boiling over with high-potential social entrepreneurs, but there are fewer of them than you might expect. Perhaps this is a result of the postwar social contracts developed in many countries, which guaranteed governments and the public sector center-stage roles in dealing with a broad array of social and environmental problems. This was true of both the democracies west of the Iron Curtain and the Communist countries of central and eastern Europe. On both sides of the now-vanished curtain, old habits seem to be taking some time to fade and die.

Finally, the smallest continent, Australia, also hosts a number of world-class social entrepreneurs, including Nic Frances, who has led such organizations as Easy Being Green, and Richard Jefferson, of Cambia. It is worth noting, however, that neither Frances or Jefferson are native-born Australians—the first arrived from the United Kingdom in 2000, the latter from the United States in 1990.

So what makes some countries and regions more successful in spawning social entrepreneurs? It is a combination of major challenges (as in the Indian subcontinent), relatively weak governments (though the United Kingdom and the United States are exceptions), a culture that encourages or at least doesn't stall entrepreneurship, and favorable legal and tax regimes.

NOTES

Preface

1. George Bernard Shaw, *Man and Superman, Maxims for Revolutionaries* (1903; in *Plays by George Bernard Shaw* [New York: Penguin, 1960]).

2. Allen L. Hammond et al., *The Next 4 Billion: Market Size and Business Strategy at the Base of the Pyramid* (Washington, DC: World Resources Institute, IFC, and the World Bank, 2007); also see http://www.wri.org/business/pubs_description.cfm?pid=4142.

3. Hammond et al., *The Next 4 Billion.*

4. David Bornstein, *How to Change the World: Social Entrepreneurs and the Power of New Ideas* (Oxford: Oxford University Press, 2004); Ira A. Jackson and Jane Nelson, *Profits with Principles: Seven Strategies for Delivering Value with Values* (New York: Doubleday, 2004); John Weiser et al., *Untapped: Creating Value in Underserved Markets* (San Francisco: Berrett-Koehler, 2006).

5. Fergal Byrne, "Auction Man," *FT Magazine*, March 25–26, 2006.

Acknowledgments

1. John Elkington, *Cannibals with Forks: The Triple Bottom Line of 21st Century Business* (Oxford: Capstone/John Wiley, 1997).

2. *Triple bottom line* was coined by John Elkington in 1994.

3. John Elkington, *The Chrysalis Economy: How Citizen CEOs and Corporations Can Fuse Values and Value Creation* (Oxford: Capstone/John Wiley, 2001). For more on blended value, see http://www.blendedvalue.org; and John Elkington, Jed Emerson, and Seb Beloe, "The Value Palette: A Tool for Full Spectrum Strategy," *California Management Review* 48, no. 2 (2006): 6–28.

4. Walter Isaacson, *Benjamin Franklin: An American Life* (New York: Simon & Schuster, 2003).

5. For an interesting history and discussion of the open source movement in software, see Steven Weber, *The Success of Open Source* (Cambridge, MA: Harvard University Press, 2004).

Introduction

1. J. Gregory Dees and Beth Battle Anderson, "Framing a Theory of Social Entrepreneurship: Building on Two Schools of Practice and Thought," in *Research on Social Entrepreneurship*, ed. Rachel Moser-Williams, Arnova Occasional Paper series, vol. 1, no. 3 (Washington, DC: Aspen Institute, 2006).

2. See, for example, www.blendedvalue.org.

3. David Green, conversation with authors, Geneva, 2006.

4. The Cleantech Venture Network defines itself as embracing the goal to "greatly reduce or eliminate environmental impacts and, in doing so, improve the quality of life" (see http://cleantechnetwork.com/index.cfm?pageSRC =CleantechDefined). It includes in its definition energy generation, storage, infrastructure, and efficiency; transportation and logistics; water purification and management; air quality; materials and nanotechnology; manufacturing/ industrial; agriculture and nutrition; materials recovery and recycling; and environmental IT and enabling technologies.

5. Roger Martin and Sally Osberg, "Social Entrepreneurship: The Case for Definition," *Stanford Innovation Review* (Spring 2007): 28–39.

6. Thanks go to Jennifer Schenker of *Red Herring* for her input while we were doing due diligence in selecting Rincón as the Schwab Foundation's Social Entrepreneur of the Year; see Jennifer Schenker, *Red Herring*, December 26, 2005.

7. Quotations by Orlando Rincón Bonilla are from interview by authors, Cali, Colombia, August 2005.

8. Daniel H. Pink, "What Kind of Genius Are You?" *Wired*, July 2006, 148–153, 166.

9. Maury Klein, *The Change Makers: From Carnegie to Gates, How Great Entrepreneurs Transformed Ideas into Industries* (New York: Times Books, 2003).

10. Catherine H. Clark and Selen Ucak, *RISE For-Profit Social Entrepreneur Report: Balancing Markets and Values* (New York: Research Initiative on Social Entrepreneurship, Investors' Circle, and Social Venture Network, March 2006).

11. Robert Neuwirth, *Shadow Cities: A Billion Squatters, a New Urban World* (New York: Routledge, 2005).

12. Siddiqui provides solutions to the urban poor's housing problems, drawing on the informal sector's successes with low-income housing and working with public sector agencies, and has benefited forty thousand to date. Patel and Arputham help slum dwellers in India's large urban centers own and control the organizations that provide them services. Adler's Johannesburg Housing Company (JHC) is refurbishing occupied buildings and constructing new ones in the inner city, offering a home to more than eighty-five hundred people and increasing the housing stock of Johannesburg inner city by 8 percent. JHC focuses on long-term maintenance while working with the communities around the buildings and mobilizing commercial funding for social housing.

13. Stephan Schmidheiny, *My Path*, http://www.avina.net/ImagesAvina/AvinaMyPathEnglish.pdf.

14. *Growing Opportunity: Entrepreneurial Solutions to Insoluble Problems* (London: SustainAbility and the Skoll Foundation, 2007), http://www.sustainability.com/insight/skoll_article.asp?id=937.

15. See http://www.grameenphone.com and http://www.grameen-info.org/grameen/gshakti/programs.html for more information.

16. Kris Herbst, "Business-Social Ventures: Reaching for Major Impact," http://proxied.changemakers.net/journal/03november.

17. Muhammad Yunus, *Social Business Entrepreneurs Are the Solution* (paper presented at the Skoll World Forum on Social Entrepreneurship, Oxford, March 29–31, 2006).

18. See http://www.adbi.org/files/sultan_microfinance.org.

19. Jonathan Ansfield, "The Coal Trap," *Newsweek*, January 15, 2007.

20. Peter Scholten et al., *Social Return on Investment: A Guide to SROI Analysis* (Amstelveen, Netherlands: Lenthe, 2006).

21. World Economic Forum, *Blended Value Investing: Capital Opportunities for Social and Environmental Impact* (Geneva: World Economic Forum, March 2006).

22. J. Gregory Dees, "The Meaning of Social Entrepreneurship," http://www.fuqua.duke.edu/centers/case/documents/dees_SE.pdf.

23. Quoted from Latin American Regional Meeting of the World Economic Forum, Buenos Aires, May 2001. Rottenberg received her undergraduate degree in social studies from Harvard and her law degree from Yale.

24. See http://ashoka.org/citizensector.

25. Bo Peabody, *Lucky or Smart: Secrets to an Entrepreneurial Life* (New York: Random House, 2005), 9–10.

26. Ibid., 10.

27. Fiona Harvey, "Branson Offers $25m Prize for Solution to Climate Change," *Financial Times*, February 9, 2007, http://www.ft.com/cms/s/e2067 f90-b867-11db-be2e-0000779e2340.html.

28. Matt Richtel, "Awarder of Space Prize to Add Others," *New York Times*, January 31, 2007.

29. Andrew Gumbel, "The Hustler and His American Dream," *Independent* (London), December 23, 2006.

30. Jennifer Reingold, "The IPO Gets Edgy," *Fortune*, February 26, 2007.

31. Gumbel, "The Hustler and His American Dream."

Chapter 1

1. Al Qaeda could be seen as one of the most effective recent examples of leverage. With funds raised from, among other things, mainstream business activities and by exploiting the latest technologies, Osama bin Laden's international network has had a huge political, social, and economic impact. As President George W. Bush put it to graduating West Point cadets the year after the 9/11 attacks: "We face a threat with no precedent. Enemies in the past needed great armies and great industrial capabilities to endanger the American people and our nation. The attacks of September 11th required a few hundred thousand dollars in the hands of a few dozen evil and deluded men. All of the chaos and suffering they caused came at much less than the cost of a single tank." See "President Bush Delivers Graduation Speech at West Point," media release, June 1, 2002, http://www.whitehouse.gov/news /releases/2002/06/20020601-3.html.

2. William Foster and Gail Fine, "How Nonprofits Get Really Big," *Stanford Social Innovation Review* (Spring 2007): 46–55.

3. "Public Good," Wikipedia, http://en.wikipedia.org/wiki/Public_good.

4. Bunker Roy, e-mail to the authors, 2007.

5. "F1 Hybrid," Wikipedia, http://en.wikipedia.org/wiki/F1_hybrid.

6. Rick Aubry, e-mail to the authors, 2007.

7. Thulsi Ravilla, e-mail to the authors, 2007.

8. Ibrahim Abouleish, e-mail to the authors, 2007.

9. Ibid.

10. Cristobal Colón, e-mail to the authors, 2007

11. See, for example, John Mackey, "Chairman's Letter," in Whole Foods' annual report, 2006, http://www.wholefoodsmarket.com/investor/ar 06_letter.pdf.

12. Unless otherwise noted, all quotations by John Mackey are from his "Winning the Battle for Freedom and Prosperity," February 27, 2006, http:// www.wholefoods.com/blogs/jm/archives/2006/02/winning_the_bat.html.

13. Milton Friedman, "The Social Responsibility of Business is to Increase its Profits," *New York Times Magazine*, September 13, 1970.

14. Mackey, "Winning the Battle for Freedom and Prosperity."

15. Ibid.

Chapter 2

1. Karen Lowry Miller, "Juggling Two Worlds," *Newsweek International*, November 2004.

2. Jean-Baptiste Say, *A Treatise on Political Economy*, Paris, 1803.

3. William Foster and Gail Fine, "How Nonprofits Get Really Big," *Stanford Social Innovation Review* (Spring 2007): 46–55.

4. Martin Fisher, statement made during working group discussion at Rockefeller Foundation, New York City, January 2006.

5. For an example of how to mobilize and conserve financial resources, see J. Gregory Dees, "Social Entrepreneurship: Mobilizing Resources for Success," 2001, http://www.tgci.com/magazine/01summer/social1.asp.

6. Catherine H. Clark and Selen Uçak, *RISE For-Profit Social Entrepreneur Report: Balancing Markets and Values* (Philadelphia: Research Initiative on Social Entrepreneurship, Investors' Circle, and Social Venture Network, March 2006).

7. Barry Coleman, e-mails to the authors, August 2006 and May 18, 2007.

8. Sahar Hashemi and Bobby Hashemi, *Anyone Can Do It: Building Coffee Republic from Our Kitchen Table* (Chichester, UK: Capstone, 2002).

9. See *Growing Opportunity: Entrepreneurial Solutions to Insoluble Problems* (London: SustainAbility and the Skoll Foundation, 2007), http://www.sustainability.com/insight/skoll_article.asp?id=937. The section of the report on the ten routes to money drew on early work for *The Power of Unreasonable People*.

10. See figure 2-4 in *Growing Opportunity*.

11. Quotations by Craig Cohon are from an e-mail to the authors, 2006.

12. David Charter, "Live8 Promises Ring Hollow as Aid for Poor Is Cut by £3bn," *Observer* (London), April 4, 2007.

13. Devika Bhat, "Geldof Says G8 Donors Are Missing Aid Targets," *Times* (London), June 30, 2006, 11.

14. Pamela Hartigan, "How Big Can Small Become? Lessons from Social Entrepreneurs," *Earth Times*, August 28, 2002, http://www.schwabfound.org/news.htm?articleid=35.

15. "Bill Drayton Paints a Vision of Changemaking," *McKinsey News*, September 2006.

16. Jim Fruchterman founded Benetech in 1989 as a hybrid nonprofit (model 2), and the organization has been working ever since to put technology at the service of the disadvantaged by fostering and financing technological initiatives that the market would otherwise not develop because the financial rewards were not enough to justify the R&D investment. These include machines that have delivered reading materials in a dozen languages to over thirty-five thousand blind people in sixty countries: Martus, a tool used by human rights groups to capture sensitive information abuses. For example, citizens of East Timor who perished during Indonesia's twenty-four-year occupation might have died unaccounted for, but a group of determined programmers and statisticians refused to let that happen. Using Benetech's HRDAG software tool, they were able to document over 102,000 civilian deaths in the former Portuguese colony. Earlier this year, Benetech got approval to adapt cutting-edge explosive-sensing technology to create low-cost portable landmine detectors. The technology was developed by the military and is now owned by General Electric. It took Fruchterman three years to convince all parties involved to let Benetech have access to it. Now Benetech engineers will make it better, faster, and cheaper.

17. Matthew Bishop, "The Business of Giving: A Survey of Wealth and Philanthropy," *Economist*, February 25, 2006.

18. "Charitable Giving Sets Record in 2004," Nonprofit Agendas, October/November 2005, http://www.newsletterlink.info/nx.asp?x=432-745-531-2352-5021-0.

19. "The FT Top 25 Billionaires," *FT Magazine*, November 13, 2004, 34–46.

20. Daniel Dombey, "The Billion-Dollar Memory Lapse," *FT Magazine*, August 5–6, 2006.

21. Ibid.

22. Learn more about Avina at http://www.avina.org.

23. Stephan Schmidheiny, *My Path, My Perspective*, http://www.vivatrust.com/ImagesViva/MyPathIngles2006.pdf.

24. Ibid.

25. See http://www.alcanprizeforsustainability.com/intro.php.

26. Jonathan Guthrie, "The Rock 'n' Roll Garden of Eden," *Financial Times*, July 6, 2006.

27. Tim Smit, e-mail to the authors, 2007.

28. A commonly held misconception is that the poor are used to living in filth and that, therefore, they are indifferent to waste collection services—and certainly not willing to pay for such services. Albina Ruiz, founder of Ciudad Saludable (Healthy City) in Peru, has proved this wrong, as has

Waste Concern. Ruiz has created thousands of community-based microentrepreneurs who collect the waste generated by over 3 million low-income people for a fee.

29. Jean Horstman, e-mail to the authors, 2006.

30. "About Dame Anita Roddick," http://www.anitaroddick.com/about anita.php.

31. Adam Jones and Elizabeth Rigby, "Seeking Change on a Bigger Business Stage," *Financial Times*, March 19, 2006.

32. Ibid.

33. *Growing Opportunity*; see also http://www.landminesblow.com/.

34. Alison Maitland, "Jeff Swartz," *Financial Times*, October 6, 2003.

35. Jane Nelson and Beth Jenkins, "Investing in Social Innovation: Harnessing the Potential of Partnerships Between Corporations and Social Entrepreneurs," working paper 20, John F. Kennedy School of Government, Harvard University, March 2006.

36. Quotations by Jonathan Shopley are from John Elkington, "Venture Capitalists Join Carbon Rush," *SustainAbility Radar*, Carbon Issue, June 2006, 10–13.

37. As one of our interviewees noted in response to this point: "Here is the elephant in the room. Let's talk about the nature of foundation boards. This question reflects the thinking of foundation boards about their own personal clout and their attention levels. When a particular foundation took a capacity-building approach, the staff found the biggest challenge was managing the board's boredom level. It just wasn't very exciting to see a list of performance indicators making an incremental and upward change. The board got bored. The program officer developed a way to utilize the board members as development consultants with the grantees, and this helped to stem the boredom tide. Understanding the motivation and stimulation of foundation board members is key to working on [on this attention span problem]."

38. For a review of the Global Exchange for Social Investment's early evolution, see Pamela Hartigan, "Delivering on the Promise of Social Entrepreneurship: Challenges Faced in Launching a Global Social Capital Market," in *Social Entrepreneurship: New Models of Sustainable Social Change*, ed. Alex Nicholls (Oxford: Oxford University Press, 2006), 329–355.

39. Muhammad Yunus, "Nobel Lecture," December 10, 2006, http://nobelprize.org/nobel_prizes/peace/laureates/2006/yunus-lecture-en.html.

40. Linklaters, with the Schwab Foundation for Social Entrepreneurship, "Fostering Social Entrepreneurship: Legal, Regulatory and Tax Barriers," January 2006, http://www.linklaters.com/community/Schwabsummary.pdf.

Chapter 3

1. "What are the Millennium Development Goals?" http://www.un.org /millenniumgoals/.

2. Mark Turner, "Slums on the Rise as People Gravitate to Cities," *Financial Times*, June 16, 2006.

3. Quotations by Rick Surpin from interview with Pamela Hartigan, New York, April 2007, and e-mail to the authors, May 29, 2007.

4. Teresa Tritch, "The Rise of the Super-Rich," *New York Times*, July 19, 2006.

5. Joseph Kahn, "China's Elite Learn to Flaunt It While the Landless Weep," *New York Times*, December 25, 2004.

6. Jeroo Billimoria, e-mail to the authors, May 25, 2007.

7. Fazle Abed, e-mail to the authors, May 24, 2007.

8. "World Poverty, Hunger and Famine: How They Fit Together," Bread for the World, http://www.bread.org/learn/global-hunger-issues/famine .html.

9. Personal interview with Pamela Hartigan, July 18, 2005.

10. Allen L. Hammond et al., *The Next 4 Billion: Market Size and Business Strategy at the Base of the Pyramid* (Washington, DC: World Resources Institute, IFC, and the World Bank, 2007).

11. Michael Laser, "He's a Light to the World's Poor," *New York Times*, May 8, 2005.

12. Ibid.

13. Pamela Hartigan, "Fabio Rosa," Schwab Foundation for Social Entrepreneurship, http://www.schwabfound.org/schwabentrepreneurs.htm?schw abid=490&extended=yes.

14. Fabio Rosa, e-mail to authors, 2007.

15. For more on the north-south divide—and the universality of environmental concerns—visit Google and do a search for "environmental + divide."

16. Quoted in Yann Arthus-Bertrand, *The Earth from the Air* (London: Thames & Hudson, 2000).

17. Quotations by Wangari Maathai are from Wangari Maathai, *Unbowed: A Memoir* (New York: Random House, 2006).

18. Ibid.

19. Ibid.

20. "The World Health Report 2005—Make Every Mother and Child Count," World Health Organization, 2005, http://www.who.int/whr/2005 /en.

21. "New Study Examines Impact of Climate Change on Health," Global Health Council, December 11, 2003, http://www.globalhealth.org/sources /view.php3?id=690.

22. Tracy Kidder, *Mountains Beyond Mountains: The Quest of Dr. Paul Farmer, A Man Who Would Cure the World* (New York: Random House, 2004).

23. Vera Cordeiro, e-mail to the authors, May 27, 2007.

24. Joni Seager, "Natural Disasters Expose Gender Divides," York University Faculty of Environmental Studies, September 14, 2005, http://www .yorku.ca/fes/fesnews/seager_naturaldisasters.asp.

25. Pamela Hartigan, "Wu Qing," Schwab Foundation for Social Entrepreneurship, http://www.schwabfound.org/schwabentrepreneurs.htm?sch wabid=767&extended=yes.

26. Wu Qing, e-mail to the authors, May 24, 2007.

27. Kofi Annan, ITU Telecom Exhibition opening ceremony, Geneva, October 9, 1999.

28. Rodrigo Baggio, e-mail to the authors, May 23, 2007.

29. "e-inclusion," http://www.hp.com/e-inclusion/en/index.html.

30. Larry Elliot, "Rich Spend 25 Times More on Defence Than on Aid," *Guardian*, July 6, 2005, http://www.guardian.co.uk/g8/story/0,,15222 26,00.html.

31. Roula Khalaf, "Hizbollah Hopes to Engineer a Quick Recovery," *Financial Times*, August 28, 2006.

32. "Pioneer Human Services," *Fast Company*, http://www.fastcom pany.com/social/2007/profiles/profile29.html.

33. Ibid.

34. Muhammad Yunus, "Nobel Lecture," December 10, 2006, http:// nobelprize.org/nobel_prizes/peace/laureates/2006/yunus-lecture-en.html.

Chapter 4

1. Muhammad Yunus, "Nobel Lecture,", December 10, 2006, http:// nobelprize.org/nobel_prizes/peace/laureates/2006/yunus-lecture-en.html.

2. See, for example, C. K. Prahalad, *The Fortune at the Bottom of the Pyramid: Eradicating Poverty Through Profits* (Upper Saddle River, NJ: Prentice Hall, 2004); and Stuart L. Hart, *Capitalism at the Crossroads: The Unlimited Business Opportunities in Solving the World's Most Challenging Problems* (Philadelphia: Wharton School Publishing, 2005).

3. Quotations by Victoria Hale are from interview by authors, Hartigan recording, San Francisco, 2003

4. Quotations by David Green are from e-mail to the authors, 2007.

5. Quotations by Kyle Zimmer are from interviews by authors, Hartigan recording, Washington, DC, July 2006.

6. David K. Dickinson and Susan B. Neuman, *Handbook of Early Literacy Research*, vol. 2 (New York: Guildford, 2006), 31.

7. "An Assessment of the Impact of First Book's Northeast Program," poll conducted by Louis Harris for the U.S. Department of Education, Fund for the Improvement of Education, 2003.

8. E. F. Schumacher, *Small Is Beautiful: Economics as if People Mattered* (orig. pub. 1973; Vancouver: Hartley & Marks Publishers, 1999).

9. Nicholas Negroponte, *Being Digital* (New York: Vintage Publishing, 1995).

10. Initial quotations from Nicholas Negroponte are from "OLPC. Frequently Asked Questions," http://www.laptop.org/faq.en_US.html.

11. Nicholas Negroponte, e-mail to the authors, February 2007.

12. Ibid.

13. Jason Overdorf, "The $100 Un-PC," *Newsweek*, February 12, 2007.

10. Negroponte, e-mail, February 2007.

Chapter 5

1. Charles P. Wallace, "Tools That Change Lives," *Time Europe*, April 20, 2003, http://www.time.com/time/europe/hero/fishermoon.html.

2. "KickStart's Micro-Irrigation Pump," *Newsweek*, July 10, 2003.

3. Martin Fisher, e-mail to the authors, 2007.

4. Andrea and Barry Coleman, e-mail to the authors, May 18, 2007.

5. AirServ International, "Annual Report," 2004, http://www.airserv.org/Air%20Serv%20Annual%20Report%202004.pdf.

6. Previous version of the Air Serv International Web site, http://www.airserv.org/.

7. "Our History," Room to Read, http://www.roomtoread.org/about/history.html.

8. Ibid.

9. John Wood, *Leaving Microsoft to Change the World: An Entrepreneur's Odyssey to Educate the World's Children* (New York: HarperBusiness, 2006).

10. Ibid.

11. John Wood, e-mail to the authors, 2007.

12. Ibid.

13. Quotations by Rory Stear from e-mail to authors, May 12, 2007.

14. "Gillian Caldwell Turns Film Into A Force For Change," Skoll

Foundation, July 26, 2006, http://www.skollfoundation.org/media/grantee
_news/072606.asp.

15. See   http://www.skollfoundation.org/media/grantee_news/072606
.asp.

16. See http://www.skollfoundation.org/newsletter/072606.htm.

17. Gillian Caldwell, e-mail to the authors, 2007.

18. Richard Jefferson. "Science as Social Enterprise: The Cambia Bios
Initiative" *Innovations* (Fall 2007): 24.

19. Conversation with Richard Jefferson, recorded by Pamela Hartigan,
September 2007.

20. Ibid.

Chapter 6

1. Hernando de Soto, *The Mystery of Capital* (London: Black Swan,
2001).

2. Morice Mendoza, "Global Liberalization," *World Business*, May
2006, 25.

3. "About Us," Health Care Without Harm, http://www.noharm.org/
us/aboutUs/missionGoals.

4. "About Us," Transparency International, http://www.transparency
.org/about_us.

5. "Frequenty Asked Questions About Corruption," Transparency International, http://www.transparency.org/news_room/faq/corruption_faq.

6. See http://www.transparency.org/news_room/faq_ti#faqti9.

7. SustainAbility, United Nations Environment Programme, and Standard & Poor's, *Tomorrow's Value: From Risk Reduction to Value Creation*
(London: SustainAbility, United Nations Environment Programme, and Standard & Poor's, 2006).

8. One of the 2006 Skoll Foundation awards went to Mindy Lubber,
a founding board member of Ceres and its president since 2003.

9. Since its founding, Ceres has moved well beyond triple-bottom-line
reporting, following up on ideas originally developed by Massie. For example,
more than two dozen companies took action on climate change as a result of
Ceres's 2003 summit, and its 2005 event produced a 10-point call for action
that included a $1 billion investor commitment to clean energy technology.

10. Quotations by Bob Massie are from Robert Massie, speech delivered at Global Reporting Initiative's G3 Launch Dinner, October 5, 2006,
http://www.ceres.org/news/news_item.php?nid=239.

11. John Elkington, "Paul Rice: Fairtrade Guerilla," *SustainAbility
Radar*, April–May 2004.

12. Ibid.

13. Pamela Hartigan, "Democratizing Knowledge and Human Capacity: Key Elements for Sustainable Development provided by social entrepreneurs," *Earth Times*, August 31, 2002, http://www.schwabfound.org/news .htm?articleid=39.

14. "Overview," Chicago Climate Exchange, http://www.chicagoclima tex.com/content.jsf?id=821/

15. Quoted in L. Hunter Lovins, "Can One Person Change the World? You Bet," *ClimateBiz*, July 7, 2004, http://www.climatebiz.com/sections/news _detail.cfm?NewsID=26897.

16. Ibid.

17. Steven D. Lydenberg, Alice Tepper Marlin, and Sean O'Brien Strub, *Rating America's Corporate Conscience: A Provocative Guide to the Companies Behind the Products You Buy Every Day* (Boston: Addison-Wesley, 1986).

18. Tessa Tennant, e-mail to the authors, August 27, 2007.

19. See http://www.cdproject.net. In terms of funding, the Carbon Disclosure Project is a special project of Rockefeller Philanthropy Advisors, with 501(c)3 charitable status, for the sole purpose of providing a coordinating secretariat for the participating funders and investors. The organization is funded by the Carbon Trust (UK), the Climate Initiatives Fund (UK), the Esmée Fairbairn Foundation (UK), the Home Foundation (Holland), the Nathan Cummings Foundation (U.S.), the Network for Social Change (UK), the Rockefeller Brothers Fund (U.S.), Rufus Leonard (UK), the Turner Foundation (U.S.), the W. Alton Jones Foundation (U.S.), and the World Wide Fund for Nature (UK).

20. "Carbon Disclosure Project Press Release," Carbon Disclosure Project, 1 February, 2007, http://www.cdproject.net/viewrelease.asp?id=9.

21. See http://www.asria.org/asria/intro.

22. Tessa Tennant, e-mail to the authors, August 27, 2007.

23. Fiona Harvey and Kate Burgess, "Renewable Energy Begins to Pick Up Speed as an Investment, *Financial Times*, January 3, 2007.

24. Ibid.

25. Quotations by Jed Emerson are from John Elkington, Silo-Buster, *SustainAbility Radar*, October–November 2003, 20–21. See also http://www .blendedvalue.org.

26. Chris Corps, in comments to the Alberta Chapter of Canada Green Building Council's Sustainable Building Symposium, Alberta, May 31, 2006.

27. Chris Corps, e-mail to the authors, August 2007.

Chapter 7

1. Brundtland Commission, *Our Common Future* (Oxford: Oxford Paperbacks, 1987).

2. According to the report, "Sustainable development is development that meets the needs of the present without compromising the ability of future generations to meet their own needs." Brundtland Commission, *Our Common Future.*

3. Ben Kage, "Coal Emissions Blanket China With Pollution," News Target.com, January 4, 2007, http://www.newstarget.com/021386.html.

4. Andreas Lorenz, "The Chinese Miracle Will End Soon," *Der Spiegel Online*, March 7, 2005, http://www.spiegel.de/international/spiegel /0,1518,345694,00.html.

5. http://millenniumassessment.org/documents.document.429.aspx.pdf.

6. Lester R. Brown, *Plan B: Rescuing a Planet Under Stress and a Civilization in Trouble* (New York: W. W. Norton, 2003); Lester R. Brown, *Plan B 2.0: Rescuing a Planet Under Stress and a Civilization in Trouble* (New York: W. W. Norton, 2006).

7. Jeffrey L. Bradach, "Going to Scale: The Challenge of Replicating Social Programs," *Stanford Social Innovation Review* (Spring 2003).

8. Assessing whether an organization is ready to scale is as important to success as determining the growth model for achieving expansion. Some of the more common choices are third-party dissemination of the initiative, a franchise model, or a more controlling headquarters-branch model. See J. Gregory Dees, Beth Battle Anderson, and Jane Wei-Skillern, "Scaling Social Impact," *Stanford Social Innovation Journal* (Spring 2004): 24–32.

9. Quotations by Mitchell Kapor are from an e-mail to the authors, 2007.

10. WWF and SustainAbility, *One Planet Business: Creating Value Within Planetary Limits* (Godalming, UK: WWF-UK, 2007).

11. Ibid.

12. Ibid.

13. Ibid.

14. Dave Berry, "World Toilet Summit Won't Lack for Seating," *Washington Post*, November 8, 2004.

15. "Joseph Bazalgette," BBC, http://www.bbc.co.uk/history/historic _figures/bazalgette_joseph.shtml.

16. "The Greening of General Electric," *Economist*, December 10, 2005.

17. Ibid.

18. Peter Marsh, "GE Looks for 'Clean Coal' Technology to Power Sales," *Financial Times*, June 19, 2006.

19. *Economist*, "The Greening of General Electric," Global technology Forum, December 14, 2005, http://globaltechforum.eiu.com/index.asp?layout=rich_story&doc_id=7890&title=The+greening+of+General+Electric&categoryid=10&channelid=3.

20. "A Lean, Clean Electric Machine: The Greening of General Electric," *Economist*, December 8, 2005.

21. "The Greening of General Electric."

22. William McDonough, "China as a Green Lab," *Harvard Business Review*, February 2006.

23. Full text of Hu Jintao's address at http://www.cnn.com/2005/WORLD/asiapcf/05/16/eyeonchina.hujintao.fulltext/index.html.

24. "The Greening of General Electric."

25. Fiona Harvey, "Jeremy Leggett: One Man's Move into the Sunlight," *Financial Times*, February 22, 2006.

26. Ibid.

27. Fiona Harvey, "Tchenguiz to Invest £1bn in 'Green' Projects," *Financial Times*, July 20, 2006.

28. Fiona Harvey, "A Good Time to Be a Green Entrepreneur," *Financial Times*, February 23, 2006.

29. John Elkington and Mark Lee, Nothing Ventured, Nothing Gained, *Grist*, April 11 2006 or see http://www.grist.org/biz/fd/2006/04/11/lee/index.html?source=biz.

30. Ibid.

Conclusion

1. George Bernard Shaw, *Man and Superman, Maxims for Revolutionaries* (1903; in *Plays by George Bernard Shaw* [New York: Penguin, 1960]).

2. James Howard Kunstler, *The Long Emergency: Surviving the Converging Catastrophes of the Twenty-First Century* (New York: Grove/Atlantic, 2005).

3. National Intelligence Council, "Global Trends 2015: A Dialogue About the Future with Nongovernment Experts," December 2000, http://www.fas.org/irp/cia/product/globaltrends2015/index.html.

4. Bo Peabody, *Lucky or Smart? Secrets to an Entrepreneurial Life* (New York: Random House, 2005), 4.

5. Ashling O'Connor, "Taking World out of Poverty by Leading It Hand in Hand," *Times* (London), July 21, 2007.

6. William C. Taylor and Polly LaBarre, *Mavericks at Work: Why the Most Original Minds in Business Win* (New York: William Morrow, 2006).

7. "BedZed and Eco-Village Development," BioRegional, http://www.bio regional.com/programme_projects/ecohous_prog/bedzed/bedzed_hpg.htm.

8. The survey was undertaken at the Schwab Foundation for Social Entrepreneurship summit in Campinhas, Brazil, in November 2004.

Appendix

1. For more information on the Schwab Foundation entrepreneurs, categorized by region, see The Schwab Foundation for Social Entrepreneurship Web site, http://www.schwabfound.org/schwabentrepreneurs_new.htm. For more on ranking the world's regions, see SustainAbility Web site, http://www.sustainability.com/downloads_public/skoll_reports/Hot_Spots_of_Social _Enterprise.pdf.

INDEX

JOHN ELKINGTON is a leading authority on sustainable development and triple-bottom-line business strategy. He was cofounder and a past chairman (1996–2006) of SustainAbility (http://www .sustainability.com); now he is the organization's chief entrepreneur. *Business Week* has described him as "a dean of the corporate responsibility movement for three decades." *The Power of Unreasonable People* is his seventeenth book. He was coauthor of *The Green Consumer Guide*, published in 1988, which sold around a million copies in twenty editions. His 1997 book, *Cannibals with Forks: The Triple Bottom Line of 21st Century Business*, was a finalist for the *Financial Times* Global Business Book of the Year Award. He is a regular columnist for publications in Brazil, China, Japan, the United Kingdom, and the United States.

Since 1974, Elkington has undertaken consultancy work for a variety of clients, including government agencies, companies, and nongovernmental organizations. He chairs the Environment Foundation and the advisory council of the Export Credits Guarantee Department. He is a member of the board of trustees of the Business & Human Rights Resource Centre and the Council of the Royal Society of Arts, as well as a member of the advisory boards of Aflatoun, the Dow Jones Sustainability Indexes (Switzerland), Instituto Ethos (Brazil), Physic Ventures (US), and zouk ventures (UK). He is also a member of the WWF-UK Council of Ambassadors.

Elkington has a BA in sociology and social psychology (1970) and a master's of philosophy in urban and regional planning (1974), and he was a 1981 Churchill Fellow. He has chaired or spoken at over five hundred conferences and major events worldwide. In 1989, he was elected to the UN Global 500 Roll of Honor for his "outstanding environmental achievements." His personal Web site is http://www.johnelkington.com.

PAMELA HARTIGAN is Managing Director of the Schwab Foundation for Social Entrepreneurship (http://www.schwabfound.org), a Swiss-based organization founded by Klaus and Hilde Schwab in 1998, which focuses on building and supporting practitioners whose efforts have achieved transformational change. The foundation is the second organization started and supported by Klaus Schwab (the first was the World Economic Forum). Hartigan is the foundation's first managing director and has been responsible for shaping the strategy and operations pursued by the foundation to achieve its mission.

Hartigan is a frequent lecturer on the topic of social entrepreneurship at graduate schools of business in the United States, Europe, and Asia. Throughout her career, she has held several leadership positions in multilateral health organizations and educational institutions as well as in entrepreneurial nonprofits. She has been responsible for conceptualizing and creating new organizations, departments, and programs across a variety of institutional arrangements and multistakeholder platforms. She is on the board of a number of entrepreneurial start-ups and more established ventures.

Of Ecuadorian origin, Hartigan received her BS in international economics from Georgetown University's School of Foreign Service, has an advanced degree in international economics from the Institut d'Études Européenes in Brussels, and earned a master's in education from American University in Washington, D.C. She received her PhD in human developmental psychology from Catholic University, also in Washington, D.C.

Coda: Late in 2007, Elkington and Hartigan were among the founders of Volans Ventures (http://www.volansventures.com), dedicated to supporting scalable entrepreneurial solutions to sustainability challenges.